Changing Lanes

Unlocking the Secrets to Freedom and Wealth
Beyond the Truck

Bill Love

Kessler Publishing
Lapeer, Michigan

Changing Lanes

Copyright @ 2025 by Bill Love

All rights reserved. No portion of this book may be reproduced, stored in a retrieval system, or transmitted in any form or by any means-electronic, mechanical, photocopy, recording, scanning or other – except for brief quotations in critical reviews or articles, without the prior written permission of the publisher.

Published by Kessler Publishing, Lapeer Michigan

ISBN: 9798300824907

Table of Contents

PREFACE 4

THE BIG WHY 7

NAVIGATING THE FUTURE OF TRUCKING 16

FROM THE ROAD TO RECRUITING 28

ROLLING INTO REAL ESTATE 40

MONETIZING YOUR EXPERIENCES WITH DIGITAL CONTENT 56

TURNING PASSIONS INTO PROFITS 73

TRADING FROM THE CAB 85

UNLOCKING DOORS TO NEW OPPORTUNITIES 112

EXPANDING YOUR PROFESSIONAL REACH 120

TEACHING AND MENTORING 132

EPILOGUE 144

Preface

"The only limit to our realization of tomorrow will be our doubts of today." — **Franklin D. Roosevelt**

In these pages, you will discover not just a series of strategies but a new perspective on securing a future that goes beyond the demanding life in the truck.

Having spent over two decades in the trucking industry, I've witnessed firsthand the challenges and rewards of life on the road. Yet, it's the untold stories of struggle, the missed family gatherings, and the yearning for stability that pushed me to explore and eventually master avenues like real estate and digital marketing. This book is my way of handing over the keys to a new kingdom—where security doesn't mean sacrificing your life… but steering it on your terms.

Imagine being able to attend every family milestone, or invest in your child's future without worrying about the next paycheck. This isn't just a dream; it's a potential reality with the right tools and knowledge. I've seen fellow drivers like Mark, who felt trapped by the relentless schedule of trucking, transform their lives through the strategic investment tips shared in these pages. Sarah, another colleague, started her journey skeptical but now enjoys additional income from her YouTube channel, all while still navigating her routes.

The inspiration for this book also came from countless conversations with peers who felt just like Mark and Sarah—eager for change but unsure where to start. Their stories are the backbone of this book, ensuring that the advice provided is not only practical but also tested in real-life experience.

I extend my deepest gratitude to the mentors and friends who have supported this endeavor. Your wisdom and encouragement have been pivotal. A special thanks to the vibrant community of truck drivers whose resilience and curiosity never cease to inspire me.

To you, the reader, thank you for choosing to invest your time with me. This book is for those who have ever felt the rumble of a Kenworth t680 or a Peterbilt 379 and wondered if there was another road to travel—a road that leads to financial freedom and time spent with loved ones.

As you turn these pages, remember that the journey to a richer life is not just about changing lanes but about changing perspectives. Whether you are well-versed in investments or new to digital platforms, there's something here for everyone.

Thank you for embarking on this journey with me. Let's roll down this road together, discovering how your current skills and experiences can fuel your tomorrow. Keep turning the pages—your roadmap to riches awaits.

Chapter One
The BIG Why

"We cannot solve our problems with the same thinking we used when we created them. Start by asking why." – Albert Einstein

Let's have a heart-to-heart. You've been out on the road for a while, and you know how it goes—the steady hum of the engine, miles slipping by under your tires, and those quiet moments where it's just you, the open road, and your thoughts. Driving gives you time to think, doesn't it? Maybe you've been wondering what life will look like when you decide it's time to park the truck…for good. What's next? What comes after a career behind the wheel?

Those are big questions, and I'm here to tell you that it's okay to not have all the answers. What matters is that you've started thinking about them, and even more importantly, that you're open to planning for your future. Whether you've got five years left in the driver's seat or 25, one thing is certain: your career as a truck driver won't last forever.

I'm not here to overwhelm you with doom and gloom or tell you to quit your job tomorrow. Far from it. I'm here to help you start planning for what's next, step by step, while you're still doing what you do best—keeping the world moving from behind the wheel. Think of me as your co-pilot on this journey. Together, we'll map out a plan to help you transition from the truck to the next exciting chapter of your life.

Why It's Important to Plan Now

Before we dive into the "how," let's talk about the why. Why is it so important to think about life after trucking now, rather than waiting until you're ready to retire or move on? I know you're busy, and it might feel like there's no time to plan. But trust me, the sooner you start thinking about the future, the smoother your transition will be. Here's why:

1. Your Health Won't Wait

Let's be real—truck driving is tough on the body. Long hours sitting in one position, irregular sleep patterns, and grabbing whatever food is available at the TA or Loves can take a toll over the years. Maybe you're starting to feel some of those effects already: a stiff back, aching knees, or fatigue that doesn't go away as quickly as it used to.

The reality is, your body might decide it's time for a change before you're ready. That's why planning for a less physically demanding career is so important. You want to be able to step into something new when the time comes, not scramble to figure it out under pressure.

2. The Industry is Changing

Trucking isn't what it used to be, and it's evolving every day. Advances in technology, from self-driving trucks to automated logistics systems, are reshaping the industry. While drivers like you are still in high demand, the landscape might look very different in 10 or 20 years.

What if you had a backup plan? What if, instead of worrying about the changes ahead, you could embrace them as an opportunity to grow and try something new? By preparing now, you'll be ready to pivot when the time comes, no matter what happens in the industry.

3. Your Dreams Matter

Let me ask you something: What do you dream about when

you're on those long hauls? Is it spending more time with your family? Starting a business? Traveling for fun instead of work? Those dreams are important, and they're worth planning for.

You've worked hard your whole life. You deserve to create a future that gives you the time, freedom, and resources to enjoy the things that matter most to you. The sooner you start working toward those dreams, the closer they'll become.

The Future Isn't as Far Off as It Seems

The thing about the future is that it sneaks up on you. One moment, you're in the thick of your daily routine—focused on deadlines, schedules, and the task at hand. The next, you look up, and it feels like years have slipped by in the blink of an eye.

It's a common experience for everyone, not just drivers. But for you, with so much time spent on the road, the days and weeks can blur together even faster. The miles roll by, the odometer climbs, and before you know it, the seasons have changed. If there's one lesson I want you to take to heart, it's this: the future isn't some distant, hazy idea. It's closer than you think, and the time to start preparing for it is now.

To show you what I mean, let me tell you a story about a

man named Eddie.

When Tomorrow Becomes Today

Eddie was a OTR driver. He loved the road—the freedom, the solitude, and the satisfaction of knowing he was doing important work. He'd been driving for 20 years and had the kind of experience and know-how that made him a pro. He could handle tight deadlines, navigate tricky routes, and keep his cool in even the worst traffic jams.

But Eddie had a habit of brushing off thoughts about the future. He'd tell himself, *I've got time. I'll figure it out later.* Retirement? That was years away. Learning a new skill? Maybe someday, when things weren't so busy. Saving more money? He'd get to it when the next big paycheck came through.

In the back of his mind, Eddie knew he couldn't drive forever. His knees ached after long stretches, and his back was stiff from years in the same seat. But he pushed those thoughts aside, focusing instead on the here and now. After all, he was making decent money, and he had bills to pay. The future could wait.

Or so he thought.

The First Wake-Up Call

One summer, Eddie's company asked him to take on more

demanding routes to keep up with increasing demand. The loads were heavier, the distances longer, and the deadlines tighter. Eddie, being the dedicated worker he was, said yes without hesitation. He figured he could handle it—he always had.

But after a few months, the wear and tear started catching up with him. He noticed his shoulders and back hurting more than usual. The long hours behind the wheel left him exhausted, and he started relying on energy drinks and other "substances" just to stay alert.

One day, while unloading part of his haul at a distribution center, Eddie felt a sharp pain shoot through his lower back. He winced but shrugged it off, thinking it was just a tweak. But the pain didn't go away. In fact, it got worse. By the time he got back on the road, he could barely sit comfortably in his seat. He pushed through the discomfort, but the experience planted a seed of doubt in his mind.

What if this keeps getting worse? he wondered. What if I can't keep driving like this forever?

A Visit to the Doctor

Eddie tried to tough it out for another few weeks, but the pain became unbearable. He finally visited a doctor, who told him he had a herniated disc in his lower back. The Chiropractor explained that years of sitting for long hours and handling heavy loads had taken a toll on his spine. If Eddie didn't make some changes soon, his condition could worsen, potentially sidelining him from work altogether.

The news hit Eddie hard. He left the doctor's office feeling shaken. For the first time, he was forced to confront the reality he'd been avoiding: he couldn't keep doing this forever. His body was sending him a clear message, and he couldn't ignore it any longer.

Back on the road, Eddie couldn't stop thinking about what the doctor had said. He started noticing all the little things he'd been brushing off for years—the stiffness in his knees, the fatigue that lingered even after a full night's sleep, and the fact that he hadn't been able to keep up with his buddies in a pickup basketball game in years.

But more than that, he started thinking about the future. He realized that he didn't have a plan for what came next. Sure, he had a little money saved up, but not enough to retire on. And when he thought about other jobs he might do, his mind came up blank. Trucking was all he knew, all he'd ever done. What else was out there for him?

For the first time, Eddie felt scared—not of the road ahead, but of what lay beyond it. He realized he had been living in a kind of bubble, assuming that everything would stay the same forever. But now, the future felt a lot closer, and he wasn't ready for it.

That night, parked at a truck stop under a sky full of stars, Eddie made a decision. He didn't have all the answers, but he knew one thing for sure: he couldn't keep ignoring the future. It was time to start planning for what came next.

Eddie pulled out a notebook and started jotting down ideas. He thought about what he enjoyed doing, what he was good at, and what kind of life he wanted for himself. He realized he'd always loved working with his hands—tinkering with engines, fixing things around the house, and even helping his neighbors with small repairs. Maybe there was something there, he thought.

Over the next few months, Eddie started taking small but meaningful steps. He enrolled in an online course on basic auto repair that he could work on during his 36 hour resets. He started saving a little more money each month, cutting back on unnecessary expenses so he could build a financial cushion. And he reached out to a friend who owned a small repair shop, asking for advice on how to get started in the field.

The Future Arrives

A year later, Eddie's back pain forced him to leave trucking earlier than he'd planned. It wasn't an easy transition—he missed the road and the sense of purpose that came with it. But thanks to the steps he'd taken, he wasn't starting from scratch. He had a plan, a new set of skills, and a vision for his future.

Eddie ended up opening his own small auto repair shop, specializing in helping other truck drivers maintain their rigs. His years of experience on the road gave him a unique perspective, and his business quickly gained a loyal customer base. Best of all, Eddie found that he loved the work. He still got to be around trucks and connect with other drivers, but without the physical toll of long-haul driving.

Looking back, Eddie realized just how quickly the future had arrived. If he hadn't started planning when he did, he might have found himself in a much tougher spot. But because he took action, he was able to build a new life for himself—one that was just as rewarding as his career on the road.

What Eddie's Story Can Teach You

Eddie's story isn't unique. It's a reminder of how quickly life can change and how important it is to be ready for whatever comes next. The future might feel far away right now, but it has a way of arriving sooner than you expect. And when it does, you'll be glad you started preparing for it today. Remember, the future isn't as far off as it seems— but with the right preparation, it can be something to look forward to. Let's get rolling.

Chapter 2
Navigating the Future of Trucking

"The secret of change is to focus all your energy not on fighting the old, but on building the new." - Socrates

Finding Stability in the Midst of Change

Tom tightened his grip on the steering wheel, feeling the steady vibration of his truck as it rolled down Interstate 40. The hum of the engine felt as familiar as an old friend, but his mind was far from the road ahead. The Dave Nemo show played softly in the background, talking about automation in trucking. Tom couldn't help but think of it as a storm cloud on the horizon, a sign of an uncertain future that was getting closer every day.

He thought back to last week's meeting with other drivers. The conversation had shifted quickly from automation to money and security. Someone had brought up "diversification," saying it wasn't just a smart move anymore—it was something everyone had to think about. Tom frowned as the words stuck in his mind. He'd been driving trucks for twenty years. The road wasn't just his job; it was part of who he was. Now, it felt like the same road was warning him about changes ahead.

Outside, the view changed from wide open fields to clusters of trees. The wind seemed to carry whispers of change along with it. Tom's thoughts drifted to his daughter, Emma. She was in college, trying to figure things out. She'd hit some bumps along the way, but she kept going, learning as she went. Maybe he could learn something new too.

The faint smell of rain mixed with the ever-present scent of diesel fuel, pulling Tom out of his thoughts. He glanced at a billboard advertising online business courses. Could that be a path forward? His heart sped up at the idea. It felt scary but also full of possibility—like heading down a new road without knowing exactly where it would lead.

As the sun set, painting the sky in shades of orange and purple, Tom pulled into the Love's and shut down for the night. He stepped out of his truck, breathing in the cool evening air. The rain still held off, hanging in the air like it was waiting for the right moment to fall. Around him, other truckers were doing the same—taking a break, catching their breath before getting back on the highway.

Tom leaned against his truck, watching a younger driver animatedly talk about investing in solar power to an older man who nodded thoughtfully. The world was moving forward, fast. Maybe it was time for him to move with it. Not to leave everything he knew behind, but to add something new to his life.

The soft hum of engines and quiet conversations filled the parking lot, a reminder of the life Tom knew so well. It was a life of long drives, endless roads, and moments like this—small breaks to think and plan. Was diversification the answer to the changes he saw coming? Could embracing something new give him a steadier future, or would it just bring more challenges?

Tom didn't have the answers yet, but for the first time in a while, he felt ready to start looking for them.

Your Future Beyond the Truck

The trucking industry stands on the cusp of a revolutionary shift, driven by rapid advancements in technology such as automation and artificial intelligence. As we navigate these changes, it becomes imperative for truck drivers to look beyond the steering wheel and consider their financial futures more holistically. The traditional role of a truck driver is evolving, and with this evolution comes an opportunity for diversification in income sources that could lead to greater financial stability and security.

In this chapter, we dive into the potential impacts of **automation and AI** on trucking, emphasizing why it's crucial for drivers to anticipate and adapt to these changes. The industry's reliance on technology could eventually reduce the demand for human drivers. Understanding this risk is the first step toward safeguarding your career.

Additionally, we cannot ignore the **physical toll** that years of truck driving exerts on the body. Long hours behind the wheel contribute to numerous health issues, which can force drivers into early retirement or unexpected career changes. Planning for longevity in any career involves acknowledging these risks and preparing for them financially.

The essence of this discussion is not just about identifying risks but also about empowering you with strategies to mitigate them. We will outline **initial steps toward diversifying your income**—a crucial move to prepare for any industry uncertainties. Whether it's investing in real estate, starting a digital venture, or exploring stocks, each option offers a pathway to generate passive income while still engaging in trucking.

Why Diversify?

The rationale behind diversifying your income streams is straightforward: it minimizes your financial risk. By creating multiple sources of income, you are less likely to feel the brunt of any single market fluctuation or industry downturn. Think of it as not putting all your eggs in one basket—an essential strategy in today's volatile economic environment.

First Steps Toward Financial Freedom

Starting this journey requires careful planning and action. It begins with exploration—understanding what options are available and how they align with your personal and financial goals. This chapter aims to equip you with foundational knowledge and practical steps that can be taken while still maintaining your current job responsibilities.

In exploring these avenues, we will also highlight how embracing change can foster not only financial growth but also personal fulfillment. Transitioning from active income dependent solely on truck driving to generating passive income streams can offer more than just economic benefits—it can provide peace of mind and a more sustainable work-life balance.

As we explore these themes throughout this book, remember that each chapter builds upon the last, aiming to guide you from understanding fundamental changes in the trucking industry to taking actionable steps towards securing your financial independence. With each page turned, my goal is to help you visualize a future where you are not solely reliant on truck driving but are thriving through diversified ventures that provide both security and satisfaction.

By embracing these strategies, you're not just preparing for a possible shift in the trucking industry; you're proactively shaping a prosperous future that leverages your skills and resilience as a driver. Let's embark on this journey together, steering toward a horizon filled with opportunities beyond the traditional routes of the past.

Understanding the Impact of Automation and AI

The trucking industry stands on the cusp of a significant transformation, primarily driven by advancements in automation and artificial intelligence (AI). As we edge closer to a future where self-driving trucks **WILL** become the norm, the role of the traditional truck driver is poised for change. This shift isn't just about technology replacing jobs; it's about the evolution of an entire industry.

Imagine a scenario where trucks drive themselves, highways are less congested, and goods are delivered faster than ever. This isn't a scene from a sci-fi movie but a potential reality that will reshape the logistics landscape. Automation promises efficiency and safety improvements but introduces uncertainty for today's truck drivers.

The adoption of AI in trucking goes beyond autonomous vehicles. It includes advanced logistics management systems, predictive maintenance, and optimized fuel management. These technologies aim to reduce operational costs and increase productivity. However, for us as drivers, it means adapting to new roles where oversight of technology becomes a key part of the job description.

In this rapidly changing environment, the need for truck drivers to adapt is clear. Those who embrace the changes can find new opportunities in overseeing fleet operations, data management, or even in training AI systems. The shift could be likened to the transformation of a caterpillar into a butterfly—a complete metamorphosis from one role to another, driven by necessity and survival in the new technological ecosystem.

Automation and AI are set to redefine the traditional roles in trucking, making adaptation and skills enhancement essential.

The Physical Toll of Truck Driving

Truck driving is more than a job; it's a lifestyle that demands long hours on the road, often leading to chronic health issues like back pain, obesity, and stress-related conditions. The physical toll of truck driving is not just a matter of comfort but one that impacts long-term health and career longevity.

The cab of a truck becomes a second home for us as drivers, where we spend numerous hours sitting and facing the vibrations and jerks of the vehicle. This constant strain can lead to severe long-term physical ailments, which might force drivers to reconsider their career paths sooner than anticipated.

Moreover, the mental fatigue from long hours of concentration and the stress of meeting delivery deadlines cannot be underestimated. It's akin to running a marathon at a sprinter's pace; eventually, the body demands a break, and without proper rest and care, burnout is inevitable.

Consider the implications of these health challenges. They aren't just personal issues but affect the overall productivity and safety in the trucking industry. A driver's well-being is directly tied to their ability to perform safely and efficiently on the road.

The introduction of ergonomically designed truck cabins

and the promotion of healthier lifestyle choices among drivers are steps in the right direction. However, these are merely palliative measures if the root causes, such as unreasonably long hours and insufficient rest, are not addressed.

Steps Toward Diversifying Income

In the face of industry uncertainties, diversifying income is like a farmer planting multiple types of crops; it spreads the risk and ensures stability regardless of external conditions. For truck drivers, this means looking beyond the wheel and exploring additional sources of income.

One practical step is leveraging skills acquired on the road. Many drivers possess deep knowledge of logistics and vehicle maintenance—skills that can be turned into consulting roles or part-time teaching positions in driving schools. Another avenue is starting a small business that aligns with your experience, such as a truck cleaning service or a roadside cafe.

Investing in learning new skills, particularly in technology, can open doors to roles in fleet management, logistics planning, or even positions in the field of AI fleet oversight. Online courses and community college programs offer accessible paths to gaining these new competencies.

Setting up a passive income stream through investments or

real estate can also provide financial cushioning. This might involve higher initial input but can lead to substantial long-term benefits. Drivers can start small, perhaps with a rental property, and gradually expand their portfolio.

These initial steps not only secure financial stability but also prepare you for a future where traditional driving roles might no longer exist.

By understanding the impact of AI and automation, acknowledging the physical demands of trucking, and taking proactive steps towards income diversification, truck drivers can navigate the future of the industry with confidence and security.

As we wrap up this initial exploration into the future of trucking, it's clear that **diversification is not just beneficial; it's essential** for your financial security. The advent of automation and AI is reshaping what it means to work in this industry, bringing both challenges and opportunities. Understanding these changes is the first step toward ensuring that you are not left behind as the industry evolves.

The physical demands of truck driving are undeniable, and they highlight the urgency of planning for a future that might not involve long hours on the road. Your health and well-being are paramount, and recognizing the toll that trucking can take is crucial in planning your career's longevity. This awareness is your safeguard, prompting you to consider alternative income streams now rather than later.

Taking those initial steps towards income diversification might seem daunting, but it is quite achievable with the right guidance and resources. By exploring new opportunities, you're not just securing your financial future but also empowering yourself to make choices that suit your lifestyle and aspirations.

Think about it: what could your life look like if you were not solely dependent on truck driving? How would your daily routine change if you had multiple sources of income? These questions aren't just hypothetical; they're a sneak peek into the possibilities that await as you turn the pages of this book.

We've laid the groundwork here, but this is just the beginning. With each chapter, we'll dive deeper into practical strategies and real-world advice on building a diversified portfolio of income streams. From investments to side businesses, we'll explore how you can use your existing skills in new ways and discover talents you didn't know you had.

Your journey towards financial freedom is just getting started, and the road ahead is promising. With a mix of curiosity, determination, and the right knowledge, there's no limit to what you can achieve. Let's steer toward that horizon together, embracing change and seizing opportunities at every turn. Here's to building a secure, prosperous future beyond the truck!

Chapter 3

From the Road to Recruiting

Can Experience Pave the Way for A New Beginning?

Jake sat at the edge of the worn leather seat in his truck, the familiar sound of the engine a comforting backdrop to his swirling thoughts. Today marked his last long haul across the dusty plains of Nebraska. The sun dipped low, casting long shadows that danced alongside his rig. Twenty years on the road had etched deep lines into his face, much like the tire tracks embedded in countless miles of asphalt.

He mused over his decision to leave the driver's seat for an office at a trucking firm's headquarters. Recruitment was a new frontier; daunting yet brimming with potential. His mind wandered to all those young faces eager and anxious as they contemplated life on the road. He could guide them, use his hard-earned wisdom to light their way. Wasn't that worth stepping away from the solitude and freedom of driving?

A sharp knock on his window snapped him back to reality. Outside stood Mel, a fellow driver whose laughter was as loud as her truck's horn. She gestured for him to join her for a coffee break at a nearby diner—a ritual they shared whenever their routes crossed.

Inside, surrounded by the clatter of dishes and murmurs of other patrons, Jake shared his plans with Mel. She listened intently, her eyes reflecting a mix of surprise and understanding.

"Man, you're jumping into some deep waters," she said, stirring her coffee slowly.

"Yeah," Jake replied, staring into his own mug as if it held answers. "But think about it—I know what makes a good driver because I've lived it. Who better to pick out the next generation?"

Mel nodded, "True enough." Her gaze shifted towards the window where trucks lined up like resting giants under the fading light.

Leaving behind their empty cups, they walked back into the crisp evening air. The parking lot smelled of diesel and cold wind; it was invigorating yet nostalgic for Jake.

As he climbed back into his cab, he felt an unexpected surge of excitement mixed with apprehension about trading open roads for office walls.

Could this transition truly keep him connected to what he loved while opening up new ways to contribute? Or would he find himself missing the freedom that each sunrise on a new highway brought?

Harnessing Your Experience

The road to riches often involves a strategic pivot at crucial intersections of our careers. For many in the trucking industry, moving from behind the wheel to behind the recruitment desk is not just a shift in roles but a significant step towards financial freedom and professional growth. This chapter delves into how truck drivers can leverage their rich industry experience to transition into driver recruitment roles, illuminating a pathway that promises less physical strain and continued industry involvement.

Transitioning from Driving to Recruitment

Imagine trading your truck cab for an office where your

knowledge fuels not just engines but futures. The move from truck driving to recruitment is driven by more than necessity; it's fueled by the opportunity to use your firsthand experiences to shape the next generation of drivers. Here, you don't abandon your roots; you plant new seeds using the same soil. This chapter will guide you through understanding this transition, highlighting what remains the same and what changes in this new role.

There are many companies that actively seek out drivers to join their recruiting team. Many of these companies offer remote work from anywhere opportunities. Apex Recruiting is a great example. They work with hundreds of different Truck driving companies. This allows the recruiter to present a driver with the best available position for them. If you reach out to them feel free to let them know that I sent you. Their website is apexdrivers.com.

Skills That Drive Successful Recruitment

What makes a great recruiter in the trucking industry? It's not just about knowing how to drive; it's about understanding what drives others. Effective communication, empathy, and strategic thinking are paramount. We will explore the essential skills that help you identify and attract top talent. From assessing technical skills to recognizing potential, this section prepares you to widen your impact in the industry without turning the ignition key.

Capitalizing on Industry Connections

Your years on the road have equipped you with more than just driving skills; they have woven you into a vast network of industry contacts. This chapter will show you how to tap into that network effectively, transforming acquaintances into opportunities. Learn how connections can be your greatest asset in securing a position in recruitment or even leading recruitment efforts within your current company.

Each step in this journey from driving to recruiting requires insight paired with action. We will discuss practical steps and strategies to make this transition smooth and successful. Whether you are looking at becoming an independent recruiter or joining an established team, there are clear pathways that can lead to success.

Embracing a recruitment role does more than open new career doors; it preserves your well-being. With less physical demands, you can extend your career duration while maintaining strong ties to an industry that has been central to your life.

Maintaining Industry Influence

Stepping into recruitment doesn't mean stepping back from influencing the trucking world. On the contrary, it positions you as a pivotal figure in shaping its future. By selecting and training new drivers, you directly impact safety standards, efficiency, and industry culture.

The shift from truck driving to a recruitment role is like a seasoned gardener who decides to start a nursery. The gardener's deep understanding of plants' needs and how to nurture them translates seamlessly into sourcing and cultivating young saplings. Similarly, truck drivers possess a profound comprehension of what the job entails, the challenges faced, and the qualities needed to thrive. This knowledge is invaluable when transitioning into a role that involves hiring and training new drivers.

Truck driving, with its long hours and demanding nature, requires resilience and adaptability. Drivers develop a keen eye for detail and a robust understanding of logistics and time management. These skills are directly transferable to a recruitment position where organizational skills and an ability to read people are paramount. The transition, therefore, is not just about changing jobs, but about leveraging existing skills in a new, less physically taxing environment.

Imagine sitting in the cab, hands on the wheel, the road stretching out ahead. This has been your world, where every turn and stop sign is familiar. Moving to recruitment is like shifting to the passenger seat. You're still on the road, but now you're guiding others, helping them navigate their paths. It's about using your journey to empower others to start theirs, ensuring they are as prepared and informed as you were.

In recruitment, your firsthand experience provides credibility. You can empathize with candidates, offering real-world advice on handling the pressures of the job. You understand what makes a good route, a reliable truck, and how to maintain focus over long distances. This role allows you to shape the future of the industry, one driver at a time.

The move from driving to recruitment is about using your road-tested knowledge to fuel the growth and success of others in the trucking industry.

Understanding the Skills for Effective Driver Recruitment

Recruitment requires more than just knowing the trucking industry; it demands a set of refined interpersonal and evaluation skills. Effective communication is the cornerstone. Recruiters must clearly articulate job roles, expectations, and feedback. They need to be adept listeners, too, understanding the concerns and aspirations of potential drivers.

One must also possess strong decision-making abilities. Evaluating a candidate's suitability involves analyzing their skills, experience, and potential fit within the company culture. It's about weighing various factors, much like deciding the best route to ensure timely delivery.

The role of a recruiter can be seen as a bridge builder. It's about connecting the right individuals with the right opportunities. This involves not only matching skills and job requirements but also fostering a sense of belonging and commitment among new recruits.

Training new drivers is another critical aspect. This involves not just teaching them about handling a big rig but also instilling a sense of responsibility and safety consciousness. The training phase is crucial as it sets the tone for the driver's career path.

Incorporating real-life scenarios in training can significantly enhance learning. For instance, sharing experiences of handling unexpected weather conditions or mechanical failures can prepare new drivers better than textbook knowledge alone.

Capitalizing on Industry Connections to Secure a Recruitment Position

Leveraging industry connections is crucial in transitioning to a recruitment role. It's not just about who you know, but about how well they know your capabilities and character. Networking within the trucking community can open doors to opportunities that might not be advertised publicly.

It's helpful to think of your professional network as a toolbox. Each connection is a tool that can help construct your new career path. By engaging with former colleagues, supervisors, and industry acquaintances, you inform others of your interest in recruitment and your valuable industry experience.

Attending industry conferences, seminars, and workshops is also beneficial. These gatherings are not just for learning; they are perfect for strengthening old connections and building new ones. They provide a platform to showcase your knowledge and interest in shifting roles.

Remember, the reputation you built as a driver—your reliability, your work ethic, your problem-solving skills—serves as your introduction before you even speak a word. These qualities make your transition into recruitment smoother, as they are exactly what employers in this new domain value.

Transitioning to recruitment allows you to leverage your on-the-road experience to evaluate and attract new talent, while industry connections pave the way for securing a position. Understanding the skills necessary for recruitment and training ensures that these new roles are approached with competence and confidence.

Shifting from the driver's seat to the recruiter's desk is a strategic move that taps into a wealth of industry knowledge and experience. Truck drivers, equipped with firsthand insights into the demands and nuances of the job, are uniquely positioned to excel in recruitment roles. This transition not only offers a career path with less physical strain but also enhances your ability to make impactful contributions to the trucking industry.

By leveraging your deep understanding of what it takes to navigate the roads safely and efficiently, you can better evaluate candidates, ensuring that only the most capable individuals join your ranks. This critical perspective aids in building stronger, more reliable teams that can uphold the high standards of the transportation sector.

The Roadmap to Recruitment Success

Step 1: Skill and Experience Assessment

Begin by taking stock of your current skills such as communication, evaluation, and mentorship. Reflect on how these can be directly applied to a recruitment setting.

Step 2: Industry Research

Investigate the recruitment landscape to understand what potential employers are looking for. This knowledge will help you tailor your approach and highlight the skills that are most relevant to the industry's needs.

Step 3: Resume Revitalization

Update your resume to emphasize your applicable skills and experiences. Make it clear why your background in trucking makes you an ideal candidate for recruitment roles.

Step 4: Networking

Expand your professional network by connecting with industry leaders at conferences and participating in relevant online communities. These connections can be invaluable as you navigate your new career path.

Step 5: Educational Enhancement

Consider enrolling in courses that focus on recruitment strategies and best practices. This will not only bolster your resume but also equip you with advanced skills to excel in your new role.

Step 6: Job Application Strategy

Utilize job boards and leverage your network to discover opportunities in recruitment. Tailor each application to reflect how your trucking experience provides you with a unique edge.

Step 7: Interview Preparation

Prepare for interviews by practicing responses to common questions in the recruitment field. Articulate clearly how your background adds value to the prospective employer.

Step 8: On-the-Job Learning

Once hired, continue to learn about the latest recruitment tactics and strategies. If possible, find a mentor who can guide you through the initial phases of your new role.

Step 9: Continuous Industry Engagement

Keep in touch with your roots in trucking. Staying informed about the industry's evolving needs will enable you to recruit more effectively and maintain relevance in your role.

Each step is designed to be actionable and flexible, accommodating the unique journeys of individuals transitioning from truck driving to recruitment. By following this roadmap, you not only change your career trajectory but also enhance your potential to impact the trucking industry positively.

Embrace this opportunity to reinvent your professional life, using your past experiences as a foundation for future success in recruitment. Your journey on the road has prepared you well; now, let those experiences propel you towards new horizons in your career.

Chapter 4
Rolling into Real Estate

Ninety percent of all millionaires become so through owning real estate." – Andrew Carnegie

Investing in Real Estate While on the Road?

Tom gripped the steering wheel, feeling the familiar cool leather beneath his calloused hands, a testament to years of work on the road. The Nevada desert stretched before him, a flat canvas where the sky and earth met in a sharp line. He'd been driving for hours, but with the sound of the engine in the background, his mind wandered far away, to a place beyond just asphalt and tires.

He recalled the conversation he had with his younger brother, John, last night. John had always been the "settled" one, that dependable guy with a house nestled in a quiet suburb and a steady gig at the local bank. Tom loved his brother, but sometimes he felt like John was living in a different world. Over the spotty cell phone reception, John had talked about real estate investments, passive income, and living the good life, all of which felt as far away to Tom as a mirage shimmering in the harsh desert sun.

The truck lumbered over a pesky pothole, jolting him back to reality. He glanced at the phone mounted on his dashboard, glowing with notifications. It displayed an array of apps — navigation tools, weather updates... and now, maybe, just maybe, property management apps? The thought buzzed around his head like a persistent fly, refusing to leave.

As he drove past a tiny town, its houses scattered like mismatched puzzle pieces, Tom couldn't help but wonder if he could really juggle such an investment from nearly a thousand miles away. He could picture the scene vividly: tenants calling him about leaky pipes or late rent while he was out on the open road, stuck behind the wheel. It felt daunting, almost ridiculous. But then again, John had talked about technology — apps and services that could handle all those headaches without him needing to be physically present, almost like having a virtual assistant who didn't need coffee breaks or weekends off.

A flickering neon sign up ahead caught his eye, beckoning him like an old friend. "Diner 24/7," it said, as if promising warmth and comfort. Tom pulled into the lot, killed the engine, and sat in silence for a moment. The stillness was a stark contrast to the whirling thoughts in his head. Inside the diner, he approached the counter and ordered automatically from a waitress, a double bacon cheeseburger, fries and a black coffee. She had a warm smile that reached her tired eyes, and he could see the weight of long shifts in her weary posture.

Tom settled into a booth by the window, his truck parked outside in the fading light, casting its long shadow. He took a sip of his coffee — strong, black, the kind that jolted his senses. Pulling out his phone, he began to scroll through property management companies. They specialized in handling everything — screening tenants, managing repairs, and solving plumbing crises. Each article was a wave of comfort and anxiety, washing over him in turns.

Could he really trust strangers with what might be his biggest financial commitment ever? The thought of wading through legal issues made his head spin, his mind racing through all the scenarios. He pictured tenant throwing huge parties, leaving him to pick up the pieces when things went south, all while he was navigating highways and dealing with dispatchers.

His coffee, steaming and rich, broke him from his spiraling thoughts. Outside, the sun dipped below the horizon, painting the desert in its magical golden hues that transformed ordinary diners into dreamscapes. The sight tugged at something in him, a whisper of hope. Maybe this whole real estate venture wasn't just a crazy idea but a path toward a more grounded life.

As twilight wrapped around him like a comforting blanket, the sense of possibility began to mingle with his doubts — maybe this could actually work if he found the right help. Tom recalled all the late-night drives, feeling lonely on the road, with only the hum of the engine and his thoughts for company. His heart ached for a change, but could he really trust technology and other people?

What would it mean to hand over control of such a big investment to others, especially when he was used to being hands-on with everything in his life? The risks felt heavy, but so did the desire for something more. He wanted "home" to mean more than just a place to park his truck at night.

With each passing truck roaring by on the highway, each driver secluded in their own cabin of solitude, Tom's resolve started to solidify. Maybe he was ready to take a leap of faith into this new world, trading in the solitude of the road for something different — a life where he could manage investments from afar, build something lasting, and connect more with family like John, who seemed to have it all figured out.

As the waitress refilled his coffee, he took a deep breath, letting the aroma ground him amidst the swirling uncertainty in his head. It was time to carve out a new path and maybe, just maybe, embrace the adventure ahead.

He took another sip of his coffee, savoring the rich taste. The waitress caught his eye again and asked, "Everything okay over there? You've got that serious 'thinking' face on."

"Just contemplating a big change," Tom replied, giving her a half-smile. "You ever think about diving into something new?"

Her eyes sparkled with interest. "Oh, you bet! I've thought about moving out of this place, maybe start my own food truck or something fun. Gotta chase those dreams, right?"

Tom chuckled, appreciating the vibe of the dinner, where it felt like dreams were being brewed alongside the coffee. "That's what I'm trying to do, too. Got a sibling who's all about that real estate life. It's got me thinking, you know?"

"Real estate, huh? That's a big leap!" The waitress leaned against the counter, clearly intrigued. "But you've got the drive for it, no doubt. You just gotta trust yourself. And if John's already in the game, you have a good coach to guide you. Just make sure you find the right company to take care of everything."

Tom nodded, "Yeah, I know. I guess I just worry about letting go of control. I've always been the type to fix things myself, you know? But I've also been on the road for way too long, and it might be time to build something that lasts."

The waitress smiled, her demeanor grounding him further. "You've got this. Just imagine that future where you can kick back in a yard after a long day, rather than staring out at headlights and highways. It sounds like your brother wants the best for you. Go for it!"

With each passing moment in the cozy diner, Tom felt each of her words sink deeper, giving rise to a storm of excitement within him. He could see it: the evenings spent grilling in the backyard, the sounds of laughter filling the air, and his truck parked in the driveway, a symbol of his journeys but now alongside a home filled with heart.

In that moment, everything clicked. Trusted management, technology, and support from John didn't seem as intimidating as they once did. Maybe he could let go a little, trust someone else to handle the day-to-day while he focused on building this new chapter of his life.

With a renewed sense of purpose, Tom decided it was time to take the plunge. He finished his coffee, reached for his phone, and started jotting down notes of the property management companies he wanted to contact. As he scrolled, he waved a heartfelt thank you to the waitress as she refilled his mug one last time.

"Best of luck with everything! I'll be rooting for you!" she called as she moved to another table.

"Thanks! You'll see my food truck out there soon too!" he joked back, a hopeful grin spreading across his face as he pictured her dream manifesting alongside his own.

As he stepped outside, the cool evening air kissed his face. His truck stood like a steadfast companion, ready to carry him on his next adventure. Tom took one last look at the fading sunset, now a soft blend of pink and purple against the deepening sky. For the first time in a while, it felt like the horizon wasn't just a limit but an invitation.

With the potential of new beginnings and the thrill of chasing dreams dancing in his heart, Tom climbed into his truck, started the engine, and set off down the road once more. This time, he wasn't just driving toward the next delivery; he was steering himself toward a future where he could have both the freedom he craved and the stability he yearned for. The open road lay ahead, but in his heart, he could already feel the warmth of home waiting just around the corner, a place to call his own and share with those he loved.

As the miles whizzed by, Tom smiled to himself. Change was scary, but sometimes, just sometimes, it was the best kind of adventure.

From Highway to Landlord: Unlocking the Door to Passive Income

Imagine managing a profitable real estate investment while cruising down the interstate. For many truck drivers, the idea of investing in real estate as a form of passive income might seem unattainable due to the nature of their job. However, with today's advancements in technology and professional property management services, it is not only possible but can be a lucrative way to build wealth without needing to be physically present. This chapter explores how you can leverage real estate as a reliable source of passive income while fulfilling your responsibilities on the road.

Real estate investment offers an attractive opportunity for generating steady income through rental properties. The first key to unlocking this potential is learning how to identify profitable real estate opportunities. This involves understanding market trends, recognizing the right locations, and assessing the viability of properties for rental purposes. By mastering these skills, you can make informed decisions that align with your financial goals.

Next, we delve into technological tools and services that facilitate remote property management. Today's digital solutions make it easier than ever for truck drivers to oversee their investments from anywhere. From mobile apps that allow you to monitor property conditions and manage tenant relations remotely, to online platforms that streamline rent collection and maintenance requests—these tools are designed to minimize your workload and maximize your investment returns.

Additionally, this chapter discusses various **strategies for optimizing rental income** while maintaining flexibility in your trucking schedule. It covers practical aspects such as choosing the right property management company, setting competitive yet profitable rental rates, and creating lease agreements that protect your interests as an investor.

By employing these strategies, you can enjoy the benefits of being a real estate investor without compromising your primary career on the road. This approach not only provides financial security but also prepares you for a future beyond truck driving.

The journey from truck driver to successful real estate investor is paved with challenges, but also great rewards. As we explore these topics further, remember that each step forward in this journey not only brings you closer to financial freedom but also empowers you with confidence and control over your financial destiny.

So let's gear up and navigate through these exciting opportunities together. Your road to riches might just have a few more exits than you expected—but each one leads closer to home.

Identifying Opportunities

Identifying profitable real estate investment opportunities is akin to finding the right gear in a truck for the road ahead. Just as a truck driver uses their knowledge of the road and their vehicle to choose the best gear, a truck driver looking to invest in real estate must use their understanding of the market to select properties that will yield high returns.

The first step is understanding the local real estate market. Researching areas with growing employment rates, low property taxes, and good schools can signal a strong demand for housing. Properties in such areas are more likely to appreciate in value and attract stable tenants.

Imagine real estate as a map of opportunities; each property is a destination. Some destinations are more popular, leading to more traffic — in real estate, this means higher rental demand. Identifying these hot spots requires looking at trends in population growth and infrastructure development. One of the easiest ways to complete this research is to start in areas that you know. No amount of data compares to the wisdom of an area you know. In many cities, the desirability of a rental property can vary from block to block.

Another crucial aspect is the economic stability of the area. A region with diverse employment opportunities and a low unemployment rate is more likely to have a robust rental market. This ensures your investment remains profitable even during economic downturns.

Properties that require minimal maintenance and are in move-in condition are typically a good starting point as a new investor.. These properties can start generating rental income immediately, reducing the initial financial strain and providing a quicker return on investment.

Profitable real estate investments are found by understanding market dynamics and choosing properties in economically stable areas with high demand.

Putting it on Cruise Control

In today's digital age, managing real estate investments remotely has never been easier. Various technological tools and services are available that allow you to oversee properties from anywhere, even the cab of your truck.

Property management software is a game-changer. It streamlines tasks such as tenant screening, rent collection, and maintenance scheduling. This software often comes with mobile apps, giving you real-time alerts and updates about your properties, which is crucial for staying on top of management tasks from the road.

Consider the analogy of a vehicle's dashboard, which provides the driver with essential information at a glance. Similarly, modern property management platforms offer a dashboard view of your investments, making it easy to monitor their performance.

Cloud storage and online document services facilitate easy access to important documents like lease agreements, tenant communication, and financial records. This eliminates the need for physical storage and ensures that you can view or share documents as needed from anywhere.

Remote monitoring systems, including security cameras and smart home technology, can also be installed in properties. These systems allow you to keep an eye on your property and ensure tenant compliance without being physically present.

Virtual tours and online listings have made it possible to market properties effectively without needing to meet potential tenants in person. This is especially beneficial for truck drivers who cannot always be available for showings.

How might these remote management tools transform your approach to real estate investment and make it as manageable as setting cruise control on your truck?

The real estate "Pre-Trip" Inspection

The first component of the Real Estate Investment Analysis Framework is Market Research. This involves evaluating the geographical areas where you intend to invest. Look into local economic indicators, growth trends, and regional demand for rental properties. This research helps ensure that you're investing in a market with a strong potential for rental income and property value appreciation.

Financial Assessment

Next, the Financial Assessment component requires calculating the total cost of investment. This includes the purchase price, closing costs, property taxes, and ongoing expenses such as maintenance and property management fees. Understanding these figures is crucial for managing your cash flow and predicting potential returns. This thorough financial planning ensures that your investments are both sustainable and profitable.

Risk Analysis

The third critical component is Risk Analysis. This involves identifying potential risks, including market volatility and the challenges of property management while on the road. By anticipating these risks, you can develop strategies to mitigate them, ensuring the stability and longevity of your investments.

Technology Integration

Finally, the Technology Integration facet of the framework showcases essential digital tools and platforms that facilitate property management, tenant screening, and real-time market monitoring. Integrating these technologies allows you to manage your properties effectively from anywhere, aligning perfectly with the unpredictable schedules of truck driving.

By employing this analytical framework, truck drivers can confidently make informed decisions regarding their real estate investments. The framework not only helps in identifying and assessing potential investment opportunities but also in managing them efficiently from a distance.

As we wrap up this exploration into the world of real estate investment from the cab of a truck, remember that the key to success lies in leveraging what is available to you. Real estate investment is not just feasible but can be highly profitable for truck drivers. With the right tools and strategies, you can manage properties and generate passive income, all while fulfilling your duties on the road.

Firstly, identifying profitable opportunities requires an understanding of the market and its trends. This might seem daunting, but with the amount of resources and platforms available today, you're never at a disadvantage. Whether it's through online real estate marketplaces or through connections made in truck stops across the country, opportunities are plentiful.

Secondly, the advancement in technology has been a game-changer. With apps and management software designed to handle everything from tenant screening to rent collection and maintenance requests, managing your property remotely is not just possible; it's also become incredibly efficient. Imagine handling most of your real estate business from your smartphone or tablet, in the comfort of your truck's cabin.

Lastly, the concept of passive income might sound too good to be true, but it's very much a reality in real estate. By employing property management services, you can ensure that your investments are well taken care of, turning them into true passive income sources. This means you can focus on driving, knowing that your real estate ventures are accruing value over time.

So, what's stopping you from shifting gears towards a

promising new career path in real estate? You're already adept at navigating the vast roads; think of this as just another route on your map to financial independence. Every mile you drive could be earning you equity in a property somewhere.

Embrace this journey with optimism and persistence. The road to riches may have its bumps, but with a solid strategy and the right tools, you're well on your way to building a prosperous future beyond the truck. Keep steering your way toward freedom—financial freedom.

Chapter 5

Monetizing Your Experiences with Digital Content

"Life is not just about finding yourself, but about creating yourself and sharing the journey." – George Bernard Shaw

Can a Road Weary Soul Find Solace in the Digital World?

Miles had always found the road to be both his sanctuary and his prison. The endless ribbons of asphalt stretched before him like the unwritten chapters of his life, each turn a new paragraph, each hill a sentence punctuated with anticipation or sometimes dread. Today, as he navigated his truck through the sprawling landscapes of New Mexico, the desert sun cast long shadows that seemed to tug at the edges of his thoughts.

Inside the cab, Miles mulled over a conversation he had with his sister last night. She had suggested he start a YouTube channel to share his journeys. "People love stories from the road," she had said, her voice crackling through the phone like distant thunder on a clear day. He chuckled softly to himself, considering how sharing could transform loneliness into connection.

As he passed an old diner that looked as though it hadn't changed since the 50s, he thought about all he'd seen. The towns that time forgot, cities bustling with life at all hours, people whose faces told stories of hardship and joy without saying a word. Could these experiences really capture an audience? The idea fluttered in his mind like an uncertain sparrow.

Miles stepped out into the cool air. He watched families and lone travelers alike stretch their legs, their faces masks of relief to be free from their vehicles if only for a moment. He imagined telling them tales of mountain passes in twilight or valleys shrouded in morning mist—would they listen? Would they see what he saw?

As he leaned against his truck sipping lukewarm coffee, Miles felt the weight of solitude press against him. Maybe this digital venture could offer more than just additional income through ads and sponsorships; perhaps it could be a bridge back to humanity from his isolated highway existence.

Could sharing these glimpses into America's heart through videos help Miles reconnect not just with others but also with himself?

From Highways to High Earnings: Unlocking the Digital Goldmine

The open road is more than a pathway between destinations—it's a treasure trove of stories, sights, and experiences unique to those who travel it. Truck drivers, with their front-row seats to America's vast landscapes and vibrant cultures, are perfectly positioned to capture and monetize these journeys through digital content creation. This isn't just about adding income; it's about enriching lives by sharing the richness of trucking adventures with the world.

The essence of this chapter lies in transforming routine drives into engaging narratives that not only capture attention but also generate revenue. The rise of social media platforms like YouTube has democratized content publication, making it accessible for everyone—including those who spend most of their days on the road. If you're a truck driver with stories to tell, this chapter will guide you through leveraging your unique perspective for both financial gain and personal fulfillment.

Life on the road as a truck driver is anything but boring. Every day brings new places, new faces, and new challenges. For many drivers, this life isn't just their job—it's their passion. But what if all those miles and stories could do more than just get you from point A to point B? What if they could help you make extra money, connect with people all over the world, and maybe even turn into a new career?

That's exactly what's happening for truck drivers who are sharing their lives on platforms like YouTube and TikTok. With just a smartphone and a little creativity, they're turning their everyday experiences into extra income—sometimes thousands of dollars a month. They're not movie stars or tech geniuses. They're regular people, sharing what they know and love, and building a community while they're at it. If that sounds interesting, keep reading. I'll show you how they're doing it and how you can too.

Starting Your Digital Platform

Before diving into the specifics of content creation, it's crucial to understand the basics of setting up a digital platform. Whether it's choosing the right equipment for filming or selecting an engaging format for your stories, *the foundation you build will dictate your project's success.* This section won't just skim over generic advice; it will provide tailored tips that consider the unique challenges and opportunities faced by someone managing content creation from behind the wheel.

The best part? You don't need a lot of fancy equipment to get started. Most drivers film with just their phones. Some don't even bother with editing—they just post their videos as-is. It's the authenticity that people love, not the production quality.

The real magic happens when you start sharing your journey. But how do you turn everyday sights into captivating content? It's all about perspective and presentation. By focusing on what makes each trip unique—be it an unexpected wildlife encounter or a panoramic sunset behind a city skyline—you begin to attract viewers who share your sense of wonder and curiosity about the world.

To you, the life of a truck driver might feel normal. You wake up, get your coffee, hit the road, and face whatever the day throws at you. But for people outside the trucking world, your life is full of mystery and excitement.

Think about it: Most people don't know what it's like to watch the sunrise over a quiet highway or navigate a tricky route through a busy city. They've never seen what the inside of a truck cab looks like, or figured out how to cook a full meal in such a small space. Even the challenges you face, like bad weather or finding a good parking spot, are interesting to someone who's never done it before.

Truck drivers who share these moments online are finding big audiences. Their videos don't have to be fancy or complicated. Some drivers post simple clips of what it's like to drive through a snowstorm or back into a tight dock. Others focus on teaching skills, like how to stay organized or how to cook on the road. There's something about the realness of these videos that people can't get enough of.

Let's look at some of the ways truck drivers are turning their experiences into online success:

- **Daily Vlogs:** One driver films their day from start to finish, showing everything from fueling up to settling in for the night. People love these videos because they give a behind-the-scenes look at what life on the road is really like.

- **Cooking in the Cab:** Another driver has built a big following by sharing recipes they cook right in their truck. From slow-cooked stews to quick skillet meals, their videos are full of tips for eating well while traveling. Not only are they making money from views, but they've also gotten sponsorship deals with companies that sell cooking gear.

- **How-To Videos:** Some drivers use their channels to teach. They make videos about how to get started in trucking, how to stay healthy on the road, or how to manage money while driving. These videos are especially popular with new drivers looking for advice.

Monetizing Your Content

Once you have an engaged audience, monetization becomes a tangible goal. This part of the chapter will explore various revenue streams such as ad placements, sponsorships, and affiliate marketing. With real-life examples from successful content creators in the trucking community, you'll learn how to turn views into revenue streams that can significantly augment your income.

Each step in this process—from setting up your channel to cashing your first check—builds upon itself, creating not just a side hustle but a potentially life-changing venture.

This journey doesn't require tech genius or marketing guru skills; it demands authenticity and a willingness to share your world with an online audience.

As we delve into these topics, remember: every mile you travel is loaded with potential stories that can resonate across audiences. Your routine is someone else's adventure. By capturing these moments, not only do you open up new revenue paths, but you also connect with people around the globe, sharing slices of life that only truckers see.

So let's gear up and explore how your trucking experiences can pave the way to new horizons in digital content creation. Embrace this opportunity to steer your narrative toward unexpected yet rewarding destinations.

How to Start Your Channel

If you're thinking about giving this a try, you might be wondering, "Where do I even begin?" Don't worry—it's easier than you think. Here's how to get started:

1.   **Pick a Platform:** Decide if you want to start on YouTube, TikTok, or both. YouTube is great for longer videos, while TikTok is perfect for quick, bite-sized clips.

2.   **Find Your Angle:** Think about what you enjoy sharing. Do you love telling stories? Showing off your cooking skills? Giving advice? Start with what feels natural

to you.

3. **Start Filming:** Use your phone to capture interesting or funny moments from your day. Don't worry about making it perfect—people love videos that feel real.

4. **Post Regularly:** Whether it's once a week or once a day, try to post consistently. This helps you build an audience over time.

5. **Engage with Viewers:** Respond to comments and questions. Building a connection with your audience is one of the best ways to grow your channel.

6. **Learn as You Go:** Don't worry if your first videos aren't perfect. Watch other creators to get ideas and improve your skills.

Creating an account on a digital platform like YouTube can seem as daunting as learning to drive a big rig for the first time. However, just as you master the gears and the roads, so too can you master the digital highway. **The first step** is straightforward: setting up a YouTube channel. This requires a Google account, which most already possess. Once created, personalize your channel by adding a catchy name—preferably one that resonates with trucking and travel—and a visually appealing channel logo and banner.

Imagine your YouTube channel as your personal broadcast station. It's a place where you share your unique experiences, just as you would share stories over a campfire. Your channel is where these stories come alive, visually and emotionally. Setting up the channel involves technical steps, but at its heart, it's about preparing a stage for your stories to unfold.

Content creation is next. This involves planning what types of videos you will create. Will they be vlogs, informational guides, or scenic compilations? Equip yourself with a decent camera and basic video editing software. Most smartphones today can shoot high-quality video, and free editing software is abundant.

To keep your audience coming back, consistency is key. Decide on a posting schedule. Whether it's weekly or bi-weekly, let your viewers know when to expect new content from you. This regularity helps build a loyal audience over time.

In essence, starting a YouTube channel as a truck driver means turning your journey into a story that others can follow. Equip yourself with the right tools, and start sharing your road experiences.

Starting a YouTube channel is as simple as setting up an account, personalizing your space, creating content, and engaging consistently.

Engaging Your Audience with Unique Experiences

When sharing your trucking experiences on YouTube, think about what makes your journey unique. Is it the sunrise over a vast desert or the bustling night markets you pass by? Capturing these moments not only enriches your content but also gives your audience a window into your world.

The key here is authenticity. Viewers are drawn to genuine content. When you talk about a particularly challenging mountain pass or a memorable interaction at a truck stop, you're offering a view into your life that can't be found in typical travel videos. This authenticity builds trust and engagement.

Consider using a rhetorical question to start your videos, such as, "Have you ever wondered what it's like to drive through the Rockies in winter?" This invites the audience into your narrative, making them feel as if they are part of your journey.

Diversify your content by adding interviews with other truckers or locals you meet. This not only varies the content but also enriches your channel with multiple perspectives.

Remember, engaging an audience is about creating a connection. Think of your content as a bridge between your world and theirs, inviting them to cross over into your experiences.

How can you use your unique perspective to turn everyday sights into captivating stories?

Let's look at some of the ways truck drivers are turning their experiences into online success:

- **Daily Vlogs:** One driver films their day from start to finish, showing everything from fueling up to settling in for the night. People love these videos because they give a behind-the-scenes look at what life on the road is really like.

- **Cooking in the Cab:** Another driver has built a big following by sharing recipes they cook right in their truck. From slow-cooked stews to quick skillet meals, their videos are full of tips for eating well while traveling. Not only are they making money from views, but they've also gotten sponsorship deals with companies that sell cooking gear.

- **How-To Videos:** Some drivers use their channels to teach. They make videos about how to get started in trucking, how to stay healthy on the road, or how to manage money while driving. These videos are especially popular with new drivers looking for advice.

So why are people so interested in truck drivers? It's simple: they're curious. Most people don't know much about trucking, and they love getting a glimpse into a world they've never experienced.

Truck drivers are also relatable. They share real stories, struggles, and successes, which makes viewers feel connected to them. Whether it's a funny story about a tough parking job or advice on how to stay healthy while driving, these videos make people feel like they're having a conversation with a friend.

Another reason trucking content is so popular is the variety. One video might show a driver cooking a meal in their cab, while the next might be a beautiful time-lapse of a sunset on the road. There's always something new to see.

Monetizing Your Digital Content

Okay, so people love watching truck drivers online. But how does that actually turn into money? Here are some of the main ways:

1. **Ad Revenue:** On YouTube, creators can make money from ads that play before or during their videos. The more people watch, the more money you can earn. Even a small channel can bring in hundreds of dollars a month.

2. **Sponsorships:** Companies might pay you to mention or use their products in your videos. For example, a truck stop chain might sponsor a video where you review their food or amenities.

3.   **Affiliate Links:** If you talk about a product you like—like a travel mug or a portable grill—you can share a special link where viewers can buy it. When they do, you earn a small percentage of the sale.

4.   **TikTok Creator Fund:** TikTok pays creators based on how many views their videos get. If one of your videos goes viral, it could earn you a nice chunk of change.

5.   **Merchandise:** Once you have fans, you can create and sell your own merchandise, like hats, T-shirts, or mugs with your brand or logo on them.

Monetizing content on platforms like YouTube can transform your trucking journey into a source of passive income. **The primary method** is through advertisements. By enabling ads on your videos, you earn money each time an ad is viewed or clicked. This requires joining the YouTube Partner Program, which has specific eligibility requirements including a minimum number of subscribers and watch hours.

Affiliate marketing offers another revenue stream. This involves promoting products or services within your videos and earning a commission for each sale made through your unique affiliate link. For truckers, this could include trucking gear, travel gadgets, or even apps useful for life on the road.

Sponsorships are a significant potential income source. As your channel grows, brands might approach you to feature their products in your videos. This type of partnership can be lucrative but requires that your content aligns well with the sponsoring brand.

Imagine each video you create as a seed planted. With proper nurturing—regular, engaging content—this seed can grow into a tree with branches of income streams from ads, affiliate marketing, and sponsorships.

By leveraging ads, affiliate links, and sponsorships, you can turn your channel into a profitable venture, enriching your journey both on and off the road.

As we navigate through the evolving landscape of digital media, the opportunity for truck drivers to monetize their unique road experiences through content creation has never been more accessible. By leveraging platforms such as YouTube, drivers can transform ordinary journeys into extraordinary narratives that captivate a global audience. This not only opens up new revenue streams but also enriches the personal and professional lives of drivers by connecting them with a diverse community of viewers.

Starting your digital journey requires a clear understanding of the content you wish to create. Reflect on your travels, the interesting people you meet, and the unique insights you gain while on the road. These elements are the foundation of engaging content that can attract viewers.

Setting up a YouTube channel is straightforward. Simply sign up, create your profile, and start sharing your stories. Remember, consistency is key. Regular uploads help maintain viewer interest and can lead to a growing subscriber base.

Investing in quality equipment like a good camera and microphone enhances your production value, making your content more appealing. Editing your videos to include clear visuals and crisp audio will keep your audience engaged and coming back for more.

Engagement with your audience doesn't end after uploading a video. Interact with your viewers through comments, and perhaps even tailor future content based on their feedback. This two-way communication builds a community around your channel, essential for sustained growth.

Finally, **monetization through ads, sponsorships, and affiliate marketing** offers financial rewards. As your channel grows, so does its potential to attract partnerships with brands, enhancing your earning capacity.

This journey from capturing footage on the road to monetizing it effectively is not just about financial gains but also about sharing your passion and experiences with the world. It's a path that offers growth, connection, and the freedom to explore new avenues beyond traditional trucking.

By following these steps diligently, you pave the way for a successful venture into digital content creation. Your unique perspective as a truck driver is not just a window into the unseen corners of the world but also a gateway to new opportunities. Embrace this journey with enthusiasm and an open mind, as each mile traveled could be the next great story to share with the world.

Chapter 6
Turning Passions into Profits

Miles away from any town, under a sky full of stars, Jack sat alone in his truck. The steady rumble of the engine felt comforting, like a soft reminder of the road he'd been traveling. The truck rocked gently, almost like it was rocking him to sleep, but Jack wasn't sleepy. Tonight felt different. He held his camera tightly, pointing it up at the stars twinkling far, far away.

Jack had been driving trucks for over 20 years, but he'd always loved the night sky. As a kid, he'd lie on the grass, staring at the stars, dreaming about what was out there. Now, when he stopped for a break during his long drives, he'd pull out a small telescope he kept in the truck. Connecting it to his camera, he'd take pictures of the stars—pictures that felt like little pieces of magic.

Last week, on a night when he felt extra lonely, an idea popped into Jack's head. What if he shared his stargazing? Maybe he could show other people the amazing things he saw in the sky. He thought about starting a YouTube channel. It seemed like a big, scary idea, but maybe people would enjoy it. Maybe they'd feel the same wonder he did.

Still, Jack wasn't sure. Would anyone really care about stars when the sun shines so bright during the day? Could his little hobby actually mean something to others?

As Jack adjusted his camera to focus on a group of stars called Orion's Belt, a sudden knock on his window made him jump. It was Mike, another truck driver who often parked nearby.

"What're you up to?" Mike asked as Jack rolled down the window.

"Just taking pictures of the stars," Jack said, a little shy but smiling.

Mike leaned in to look at Jack's camera screen. The photo showed a galaxy shining like a tiny treasure chest of lights.

"Whoa, that's awesome," Mike said, clearly impressed.

The two of them ended up talking for hours. Jack showed Mike constellations and explained how light pollution could hide the stars. By the time the first light of morning crept over the horizon, painting the sky orange and pink, Mike left feeling inspired. Jack, on the other hand, felt something he hadn't felt in a while: pride.

As the sun rose and Jack hit the road again, he thought about where this new idea could lead him. Maybe he could get sponsors or connect with astronomy groups. Maybe he could share live videos of celestial events from the cab of his truck. Maybe his nights wouldn't feel so lonely anymore.

For the first time in a long while, Jack felt like the road ahead wasn't just about getting from one place to another. Maybe his love for the stars could turn into something bigger—something that would light up not just his nights, but the lives of others, too.

From Hobby to Income: Unleashing Your Hidden Potential

In a world where traditional job roles are continually being reshaped by technology and global trends, the ability to pivot and adapt can be your greatest asset. This is particularly true for truck drivers seeking financial freedom and fulfillment beyond the highway. Imagine turning your personal hobbies into a profitable venture, all while maintaining the freedom of the open road. This chapter explores how truck drivers can harness their unique hobbies and interests, transforming them into viable sources of income through strategic content creation.

The Power of Niche Markets

In today's digital landscape, niche markets are goldmines of opportunity. As a truck driver, you already belong to a unique community with its own set of interests and challenges. Whether it's model building, photography, or even cooking on the road, your hobby has potential market appeal. By identifying hobbies that resonate with similar audiences, you can create content that not only entertains but also educates and connects. This approach ensures that your offerings have a ready-made audience eager for content that speaks directly to their experiences and interests.

Crafting Content That Connects

Creating engaging content isn't just about sharing what you love; it's about storytelling in a way that resonates with your audience. This involves understanding what makes your hobby appealing to others in your community and presenting it in an accessible and engaging format. Videos, blogs, and podcasts are popular formats that can capture the essence of your hobby while providing value to your audience. The key is consistency and authenticity—qualities that build trust and engagement over time.

Strategic Partnerships for Growth

No venture thrives in isolation. This chapter will dive into how forming partnerships with brands and businesses related to your hobby can amplify your reach and profitability. These partnerships not only provide financial backing but also enhance credibility and access to wider audiences. Learning how to attract and negotiate with potential partners is crucial, requiring a clear understanding of what you can offer and what you need to grow.

Turning a hobby into a paycheck is more than just monetizing an interest—it's about creating a sustainable business model that brings personal satisfaction and financial rewards. For truck drivers looking for meaningful engagement beyond their usual routes, this transformation offers a path filled with potential.

Embrace Change, Embrace Growth

At its core, this journey from hobby to paycheck is about embracing change. It's about seeing beyond the immediate horizon to what could be possible if you invest in your passions. With practical steps and strategic insights, this chapter aims not only to inspire but also to equip you with the tools needed to begin this exciting transition.

Your road to riches may have started in the cab of a truck, but it could very well flourish in the digital world where passions become professions. Ready to shift gears? Let's explore how you can turn those miles on the road into milestones in your new career path.

Identifying Monetizable Hobbies

When you think about hobbies, what comes to mind? Perhaps model building, knitting, or even gourmet cooking. These are not just leisure activities but can be transformed into profitable ventures with the right approach in the digital landscape. By harnessing the power of online platforms such as YouTube or Instagram, truck drivers can share their unique hobbies with a global audience.

The first step is to pinpoint hobbies that have a broad appeal or a very passionate niche following. For instance, if you're adept at crafting custom furniture, videos showcasing your process from raw wood to a polished end product can captivate an audience. This not only shares your passion but also sets the foundation for monetization through advertisement or sponsorships.

Imagine your hobby as a seed. With proper care, it grows and blossoms, much like how nurturing your interest with quality content can attract viewers and potential revenue. It's about finding that special something you do that not only brings you joy but can also bring value to others.

Cooking is another excellent example. Perhaps you've picked up unique recipes on your travels or specialize in quick roadside meals. By creating engaging content that demonstrates your cooking skills, you provide real value to an audience that craves new culinary experiences. Here, the key is consistency and presenting content in an engaging way that keeps viewers coming back.

Photography, particularly if you're often on scenic routes, can also be highly lucrative. A channel dedicated to photography tips and showcasing breathtaking landscapes can attract both amateur photographers and travel enthusiasts.

The essence of monetizing hobbies lies in identifying what you love doing and sharing it with the world in a way that captivates and engages.

Developing Targeted Content Strategies

To effectively reach and engage with niche markets, it's essential to tailor your content to meet the specific interests and needs of your audience. This begins with understanding who your audience is and what they value. Are they hobbyists, professionals, or simply enthusiasts?

Answering these questions can guide the type of content you produce.

For example, if you are creating content about DIY truck maintenance, your primary audience might be fellow truckers looking for cost-effective solutions. Here, practical, step-by-step guides that address common truck issues would be ideal. This type of content not only serves a practical purpose but also builds a community around shared challenges and solutions.

Using rhetorical questions can be a powerful tool to engage viewers. Consider asking, "Have you ever felt frustrated by unexpected truck breakdowns?" This directly addresses the viewer's potential pain points, making the content more relatable and engaging.

The specificity of your content also plays a crucial role in attracting niche markets. If you're into model trains, for instance, videos exploring different models, track setups, and custom modifications can attract enthusiasts who are searching for detailed and specialized content.

Another strategy involves collaborating with other content creators in your niche. This can increase your visibility and help you tap into an already established audience base that shares an interest in your hobby.

Imagine your content as a magnet; the more specific and

tailored it is, the stronger it attracts those who are most interested.

How might refining the focus of your content enhance its appeal to your target audience?

Cultivating Brand Partnerships

Once you have established a dedicated audience, the next step is to explore partnerships with relevant brands and businesses. This can significantly boost your revenue and provide more value to your audience. Start by identifying brands that align with your content's theme and values.

For instance, if your channel is about outdoor adventures, partnering with makers of hiking gear or outdoor cooking equipment can be beneficial. Reach out to these companies with a detailed proposal highlighting your audience demographics, engagement rates, and how a partnership could be mutually beneficial.

It's also important to maintain authenticity when promoting products or brands. Your audience trusts you, and genuine recommendations will foster trust and maintain your credibility. Think of these partnerships as a bridge, connecting your audience with products or services that genuinely enhance their experience in relation to your content.

Lastly, always be transparent about partnerships. Trust is hard to earn and easy to lose. Being upfront about sponsorships helps maintain your audience's trust and respects their right to informed viewing.

The strategic alignment of content, audience, and partnerships forms a powerful trifecta that not only enhances your revenue potential but also solidifies your credibility and influence within your niche.

Turning your passion into a profitable venture is not just a dream; it's a tangible goal that can significantly enhance your financial freedom and personal satisfaction. By identifying hobbies that can be monetized, targeting niche markets effectively, and fostering strategic partnerships, you pave a clear path toward transforming your interests into income.

From Passion to Profit: A Step-by-Step Guide

Start by identifying your hobbies that have potential for monetization. This could be anything from woodworking and painting to digital photography or cooking. The key here is to pinpoint activities that you not only enjoy but also those where you can offer unique value or perspective.

Next, **conduct thorough market research** to understand the audience for your chosen niche. Look at what similar content creators are doing and identify gaps in the market.

This research will guide you in crafting content that resonates with a specific audience, increasing your chances of success.

Choosing the **right platform** is crucial. If your hobby is visually oriented, Instagram or Pinterest might be ideal. For video-based hobbies like DIY projects or cooking, YouTube could be more appropriate. Select a platform that aligns with the nature of your content and where your target audience is most active.

Once your platform is selected, start **creating engaging content**. Consistency is key in building an audience. Develop a content calendar, plan your posts, and stick to a regular posting schedule. This consistency helps build trust and keeps your audience engaged.

Engagement with your audience cannot be overstated. Respond to comments, ask for feedback, and encourage viewer interaction. This builds a community around your content, fostering loyalty and increasing viewer retention.

As your audience grows, look for **opportunities to partner with brands**. These partnerships can provide additional revenue streams through sponsorships or affiliate marketing. Choose partnerships that align with your content and resonate with your audience to maintain authenticity.

Consider **expanding your content** into workshops or online courses if applicable. This not only diversifies your income but also establishes you as an authority in your niche.

Finally, **utilize analytics tools** to track the performance of your content. Understanding what works and what doesn't allows you to make informed decisions about future content and strategies.

By following these steps, you can effectively monetize your hobbies while enriching your life with activities that bring you joy and fulfillment. Remember, the journey from hobby to paycheck is not just about earning money—it's about taking control of your happiness and future. Embrace the process, learn continuously, and watch as your passions pave the way to new opportunities and financial growth.

Chapter 7

Trading from the Cab

"The goal of the non-professional investor should not be to pick winners but should rather be to own a cross-section of businesses that in aggregate are bound to do well."

— Warren Buffet

Can a Truck Driver Turn Market Trends into Roadside Riches?

Tom shifted in the driver's seat of his rig, parked under the cool shade of an overpass. It was midday and the sun was fierce, casting sharp shadows that sliced across the dashboard. The rumble of passing vehicles on Interstate 80 was a constant companion, yet today it seemed like a distant murmur to Tom as he scrolled through his mobile trading app. His eyes were intent on the flickering numbers, symbols of a world so different from the asphalt and diesel he knew well.

He remembered his first encounter with stock investments—a conversation drowned in truck stop coffee and skepticism. But now, with each dividend notification that pinged on his phone, he felt a growing sense of validation. There was something empowering about nurturing this supplementary income, something that softened the harsh edges of uncertainty in his line of work.

Tom's thoughts drifted to last week when he had dinner with old friends from high school. They talked about job security and retirement plans—topics that once made Tom uneasy. Now, here he was, dabbling in stocks while others clocked into their nine-to-fives. He felt a surge of pride but also a twinge of anxiety. Was this sustainable? Could he really rely on this digital income stream in an industry notorious for its unpredictability?

The screech of brakes snapped him back to reality as a car

cut off another just ahead, their tires screaming protests against the sudden friction. He sighed and placed his phone down for a moment, staring out at the open road that lay beyond the concrete barriers.

As Tom picked up his phone again to check one last stock before driving on, he wondered if others like him could find solace and security in these small glowing screens filled with potential wealth. Could every truck driver harness this strategy to pave their way towards financial independence?

Transforming Your Financial Journey While on the Road?

In a world where job security is more myth than reality, particularly in the dynamic sphere of trucking, preparing for the future has never been more crucial. It's time to explore how the stock market can become a truck driver's new best friend, offering not just a cushion, but a potential trampoline to greater financial heights. This chapter delves into why and how investing in stocks—specifically dividend-yielding stocks—can be a smart move for truckers looking to enhance their financial stability and independence.

The Basics of Stock Market Investment

Understanding the stock market might seem daunting, but it's less complex than you might think. It's essential to grasp what stocks are and how the market operates. Consider this: every time you purchase a stock, you're buying a small piece of a company. The value of these shares can rise or fall based on how well the company is doing and how investors perceive its future prospects. We'll start by demystifying these concepts, ensuring you have a solid foundation before moving forward.

Day Trading is NOT investing

When it comes to the stock market, it can feel like there's a lot of pressure to "get rich quick." You might hear stories about people making tons of money in just a few days by buying and selling stocks. This is called day trading, and while it can sound exciting, it's important to know the risks. Day trading isn't the same as long-term investing, and it comes with some big pitfalls that many people don't realize until it's too late.

If you're thinking about getting into the stock market, understanding the difference between day trading and long-term investing is key. Personally I am not a fan of Day Trading and as a truck driver your focus during the day should be on driving down the road not looking at stock charts. There is ample opportunity to make significant financial gains without looking at the market minute by minute. Let's break it down in a way that's simple, friendly, and easy to understand.

Day trading is when someone buys and sells stocks or other investments within the same trading day. The goal is to make money from small, quick changes in the prices of stocks. For example, a stock might start the day at $50 and rise to $52 by noon. A day trader might buy the stock at $50 in the morning and sell it at $52 a few hours later, making a $2 profit per share.

But here's the catch: day trading is not as easy as it sounds. It's a fast-paced, high-pressure activity that requires constant attention to the stock market. Day traders often make dozens of trades a day, trying to take advantage of small price movements. They use tools like stock charts, market news, and technical indicators to decide when to buy or sell. The problem is, no one can predict stock prices perfectly, so even the best day traders lose money sometimes.

The Pattern Day Trading Rule

If you're thinking about day trading, there's an important rule you need to know: the **Pattern Day Trading Rule** (PDT rule). This rule applies to anyone trading in a margin account (an account where you can borrow money to trade). Here's how it works:

- A **pattern day trader** is someone who makes **four or more day trades in a rolling five-business-day period**.

- If you're flagged as a pattern day trader, you must maintain a **minimum account balance of $25,000** in your margin account.

- If your account falls below $25,000, you won't be allowed to make any more day trades until you bring your balance back up.

This rule is in place to protect investors. Day trading is risky, and having a higher account balance helps ensure traders can handle potential losses. However, it also means that day trading isn't accessible to everyone. If you don't have $25,000 to put into your account, you won't be able to day trade frequently.

Day traders often focus on highly volatile stocks—these are stocks that move up and down a lot in a single day. They might buy a stock when it dips and sell it when it rises, trying to capture quick profits. Some day traders also use strategies like:

- **Scalping:** Making very quick trades, often holding a stock for just minutes or even seconds, to earn small profits repeatedly throughout the day.

- **Momentum Trading:** Buying stocks that are moving sharply in one direction (up or down) and trying to ride the wave of momentum.

- **Short Selling:** Betting that a stock's price will go down. Traders sell shares they don't own and buy them back later at a lower price, pocketing the difference.

Day trading often requires fancy software, fast internet, and a deep understanding of how the market works. Many day traders also pay for real-time data feeds and tools to track stock movements. All of this adds to the cost of day trading, making it even harder to turn a profit.

The Risks of Day Trading

One of the biggest challenges of day trading is how quickly things can change. Stock prices can jump or drop in seconds, and if you're not paying close attention, you could lose money fast. Even professional traders with years of experience struggle to make consistent profits.

Day trading also requires a lot of time. To succeed, you have to spend hours each day watching the market, analyzing data, and making decisions. This can be stressful and exhausting, especially if you're juggling other responsibilities like a full-time job or family.

The PDT rule adds another layer of difficulty. If you don't have $25,000 to maintain in your account, you could find yourself locked out of day trading after just a few trades. Even if you do have enough money, there's no guarantee you'll make a profit. In fact, studies show that most day traders lose money in the long run.

Day trading might sound exciting, but it's important to understand what you're getting into. Between the risks, costs, and the restrictions of the PDT rule, it's not a simple or easy way to make money. Many people find that the stress and effort of day trading aren't worth the potential rewards. Instead, they turn to long-term investing, which offers a steadier, less risky path to building wealth.

Why Long-Term Investing Works

Long-term investing is one of the most proven ways to build wealth over time. It's the strategy of buying investments, like stocks or index funds, and holding onto them for years or even decades. While day trading relies on fast decisions and short-term market movements, long-term investing focuses on patience and growth. It's a slow and steady approach, but one that has helped countless people achieve financial security and even wealth.

Let's dive deeper into why long-term investing works, breaking it down into key reasons with more details and examples for each.

1. The Power of Time and Compounding

Time is your greatest ally when it comes to investing. The longer you leave your money in the market, the more time it has to grow, thanks to a concept called **compounding**. Compounding is when the returns you earn on your investments start earning returns themselves. This creates a snowball effect, where your money grows faster and faster over time.

- **Example of Compounding:** Imagine you invest $1,000 in the stock market, and it grows by 10% in a year (the historical average return for the stock market). At the end of the year, you have $1,100. The next year, if the market grows another 10%, your investment grows not just on the original $1,000, but also on the $100 you earned last year. Now you have $1,210. Over 20 or 30 years, this small growth adds up to a significant amount of money.

The key to compounding is patience. The earlier you start investing, the more time your money has to grow. Even small amounts invested early can grow into a large sum over decades. For example, someone who invests $50 a month starting at age 25 could end up with more money by retirement than someone who invests $200 a month starting at age 40, simply because the first person gave their money more time to compound.

2. Less Stress About Market Fluctuations

One of the biggest challenges of day trading is dealing with the constant ups and downs of the market. Prices can swing wildly from one moment to the next, and day traders need to be glued to their screens, making split-second decisions. This can be incredibly stressful and exhausting.

Long-term investors, on the other hand, don't need to worry about these short-term movements. Instead of focusing on what the market is doing today or tomorrow, they focus on the big picture. Over the long term, the stock market has historically gone up, despite short-term downturns.

- **Example of Market Resilience:** If you look at a chart of the U.S. stock market over the last 100 years, you'll see it includes many crashes and bear markets (times when stocks drop significantly). But after every crash, the market has recovered and gone on to reach new highs. Investors who stayed the course and didn't sell during these downturns often saw their investments grow even more in the recovery.

By focusing on the long term, you avoid the stress of trying to time the market perfectly. Even if there's a bad year or two, history shows that the market tends to recover and grow over time.

3. Simplicity and Accessibility

Long-term investing doesn't require fancy tools, in-depth knowledge of stock charts, or constant attention. It's a straightforward strategy that anyone can follow, even if they're new to investing.

- **Index Funds for Simplicity:** One of the easiest ways to invest for the long term is through index funds. These are collections of stocks that represent a specific market, like the S&P 500. When you invest in an index fund, you're essentially buying a small piece of every company in that index. This means you don't have to worry about picking individual stocks. If the overall market goes up, your investment grows with it.

- **Dollar-Cost Averaging:** Long-term investing also allows you to use a simple strategy called **dollar-cost averaging**. This means investing a set amount of money regularly, like every month, no matter what the market is doing. This takes the guesswork out of investing and helps you avoid the temptation to time the market. Over time, this strategy smooths out the ups and downs and can lead to solid returns.

Because long-term investing is so simple, it's accessible to almost everyone. You don't need to be an expert or have a lot of money to start. Many platforms let you begin with just a few dollars, making it easy to build good investing habits early.

4. Owning a Piece of Successful Businesses

When you invest in stocks, you're buying a small piece of a company. This means you're sharing in the success of the businesses you invest in. If the company grows, expands, and makes more money, the value of your stock increases. Over time, this can lead to significant returns.

- **Example of Growth Stocks:** Think about companies like Apple, Amazon, or Microsoft. Investors who bought shares in these companies years ago and held onto them have seen massive growth in their investments. For example, someone who bought Amazon stock in 2000 and held onto it for 20 years could have seen their initial investment grow by thousands of percent.

The beauty of long-term investing is that you don't have to pick the next Amazon or Apple to succeed. By investing in a diversified portfolio of stocks or an index fund, you're likely to benefit from the overall growth of the market.

5. Historical Success of Long-Term Investing

One of the strongest arguments for long-term investing is its proven track record. Over the last century, the stock market has delivered an average annual return of around 7-10% after adjusting for inflation. While there are bad years and good years, the overall trend has been upward.

- **Case Study:** During the 2008 financial crisis, the

market dropped by about 50%, and many investors panicked and sold their stocks. However, those who stayed invested saw the market recover within a few years and go on to reach new highs. By 2020, the market had grown significantly beyond its pre-crisis levels, rewarding patient investors.

This historical growth makes long-term investing one of the safest and most reliable ways to build wealth over time.

6. Tax Advantages of Holding Investments

Long-term investing also comes with tax benefits. When you sell a stock that you've held for more than a year, the profit is taxed at a lower rate than if you sell it within a year. This is called the **long-term capital gains tax rate**, and it's designed to encourage people to invest for the long term.

For example, if you're in the 15% tax bracket for long-term capital gains, you'll pay significantly less tax on your profits compared to someone who sells stocks frequently and pays the higher short-term rate. This means more of your money stays invested, helping it grow even more.

7. Building Wealth Without Constant Effort

One of the best things about long-term investing is that it doesn't require constant effort. Once you've chosen your investments and set up a regular investing schedule, you can let your money work for you. This is what makes long-term investing such a great option for busy people who don't have time to watch the market every day.

- **Automation:** Many investment platforms allow you to automate your contributions, so you don't even have to think about it. For example, you can set up an automatic transfer from your bank account to your investment account every month. This makes it easy to stay consistent and build wealth over time.

- **Set It and Forget It:** Unlike day trading, where you need to make constant decisions, long-term investing lets you "set it and forget it." You can focus on other areas of your life while your investments grow in the background.

8. Resilience in Tough Times

Life isn't always smooth sailing, and neither is the stock market. But long-term investing teaches you to be resilient. Instead of panicking when the market goes down, you learn to see it as an opportunity. In fact, many experienced investors view market downturns as a chance to buy stocks at a discount.

- **Market Recovery:** History shows that the market has always recovered from downturns. If you stay invested and even continue buying during tough times, you can come out ahead when the market rebounds.

Patience Pays Off

Long-term investing works because it's built on patience, consistency, and the power of time. Unlike day trading, it doesn't rely on guessing what the market will do tomorrow. Instead, it focuses on the big picture—letting your money grow steadily over years or decades.

By starting small, staying consistent, and focusing on quality investments, anyone can succeed with long-term investing. It's not about being the smartest person in the room or timing the market perfectly. It's about having a plan, sticking to it, and letting time do the heavy lifting.

So, plant those seeds today. With time, care, and patience, your investments can grow into something truly life-changing.

Dividend Stocks as a Source of Regular Income

One of the most attractive options for truckers is investing in dividend stocks. These are shares of companies that pay regular dividends—essentially sharing a portion of their profits with shareholders. For truck drivers, who may not always have consistent schedules or income streams, receiving dividends can provide regular supplementary income. This chapter will guide you through selecting robust dividend stocks that align with your long-term financial goals.

Picking Your First Stock: Start with a Company You Know

So, you're thinking about buying your first stock—congratulations! Investing in the stock market is a fantastic way to grow your money over time. But let's face it: getting started can feel a little overwhelming. There are so many companies, numbers, and news stories about stocks going up and down. You might even feel like you need a finance degree or years of experience to figure it all out. But the truth is, you don't have to know everything to make a smart investment.

One of the simplest and best ways to start is by picking a company you already know and trust. Think about it—every day, you interact with businesses that you give your money to. Maybe you grab a coffee at Starbucks, swing through the McDonald's drive-thru for a quick lunch, or stop by Dutch Bros Coffee for an afternoon pick-me-up. These are companies you already believe in because you're a customer, and chances are, lots of other people are too.

One of the best parts of this approach is how it helps you stay calm when things get tough. Let's say you've bought Starbucks stock, and suddenly, the price dips. At first, you might feel worried—did you make a mistake? But then you think about the Starbucks down the street. It's still packed with people ordering lattes and iced coffees. You realize the business isn't going anywhere, and the dip is just part of the market's normal ups and downs.

The same goes for McDonald's. If their stock price falls for a week or two, does that mean the company is failing? Not necessarily. You can drive by and see the Golden Arches lit up, with cars lined up for nuggets and fries. That reminder of the company's real-world success can give you the confidence to stick with your investment, even when things get a little rocky.

The idea here is simple: start with something you know, something you trust, and something you believe in. Investing can feel intimidating at first, but when you choose a company you're already familiar with, it becomes more personal and less mysterious. You're not just buying stock; you're becoming a part-owner in a business you love. And that's a great way to begin your journey as an investor.

Truck Drivers have an Advantage

Being a truck driver offers a unique perspective on the economy that most people don't have. As you travel the country and haul loads, you're at the heart of what keeps businesses moving—literally. One of the biggest benefits of being a truck driver is that you gain first-hand insights into which companies are thriving and which ones are struggling, all based on freight volumes and the patterns you notice along your routes. This can be incredibly useful if you're considering investing in the stock market or simply want a better understanding of the economy.

As a truck driver, you're directly involved in transporting the goods that businesses produce and sell. This gives you an up-close view of how busy companies are. When certain businesses are shipping large volumes consistently, it's a good sign they're doing well. For example, if you're regularly hauling loads for a big-box retailer or a popular food brand, it might indicate that their products are in high demand. On the other hand, if shipments for a company slow down or become irregular, it could mean they're facing challenges.

Your observations of freight volumes aren't just numbers; they're a real-world indicator of how industries and companies are performing. This gives you insights that many investors or analysts who sit behind desks don't have. You're out there on the front lines, seeing which warehouses are bustling and which are nearly empty.

One of the most valuable parts of being a truck driver is your exposure to different industries. You might haul everything from consumer goods to building materials, food, or high-tech equipment. This gives you a broad understanding of the economy. For example:

- **Retail and Consumer Goods**: If you notice a

surge in loads going to major retailers during certain times of the year, it could indicate strong consumer spending. Conversely, a noticeable drop in shipments could signal challenges in the retail sector.

- **Construction and Manufacturing**: Hauling materials like steel, lumber, or heavy machinery gives you insight into how active the construction and manufacturing sectors are. High volumes often mean growth, while a slowdown might signal trouble.

- **E-commerce**: Delivering packages for companies like Amazon or other online retailers can provide clues about the strength of the e-commerce industry. If fulfillment centers are busier than ever, it's a sign that online shopping is thriving.

By paying attention to these trends, you're essentially gathering data that can help you make smarter decisions about investing or understanding the bigger picture of how the economy is doing.

Adapting to Market Changes

Freight volumes also reveal how quickly companies and industries adapt to changing market conditions. For example, during busy holiday seasons, you might notice an increase in shipments for certain businesses. But if a company doesn't seem to scale up during these peak times, it could mean they're struggling to keep up with demand. Alternatively, during slower economic periods, you might see which companies continue to ship consistently, showing their resilience.

As a truck driver, you're able to spot these shifts early. This kind of awareness is incredibly valuable, whether you're looking to invest in stocks, start a side business, or simply better understand where the economy is headed.

In conclusion, being a truck driver isn't just about delivering goods—it's about having a front-row seat to the economy. Your observations of freight volumes and industry patterns can provide valuable insights into which businesses are succeeding and which ones aren't. This knowledge can give you an edge in making smarter financial choices, whether you're investing in stocks or simply planning for your future. So, the next time you're behind the wheel, remember: you're not just driving a truck; you're witnessing the economy in motion.

Buying Your First Stock: A Step-by-Step Guide

Thanks to technological advancements, trading no longer requires being glued to a computer screen in an office. Mobile trading platforms have revolutionized the way we invest, allowing anyone with a smartphone and an internet connection to manage their portfolio from anywhere—at home, on a break, or even while sitting in your truck cab during a rest stop. We'll explore how to utilize these tools effectively, ensuring you can monitor and manage your investments seamlessly without disrupting your primary job.

Buying your first stock might seem complicated, but it's actually much simpler than you think. With a bit of preparation and the right mindset, you can go from being a curious beginner to an investor in just a few steps. In this section, we'll walk through everything you need to know, from choosing the right platform to making your first purchase. By the end, you'll feel confident and ready to dive into the world of investing.

Step 1: Understand What It Means to Own a Stock

Before we jump into the mechanics of buying your first stock, let's start with the basics: what is a stock? When you buy a share of stock, you're purchasing a small piece of ownership in a company. For example, if you buy stock in Starbucks, you're not just a customer anymore—you're also a part-owner. As an owner, you benefit when the company does well because the value of your stock can go up, and sometimes you even earn a share of the profits through dividends.

Owning stock gives you a stake in a business's success,

which is why picking a company you believe in and understand is so important. You're not just buying a piece of paper or a number on a screen; you're becoming a part of something bigger.

Step 2: Choose a Brokerage Account

To buy stock, you'll need to open a brokerage account. A brokerage is like a middleman that connects you to the stock market. The good news is that opening an account is easier than ever, thanks to online platforms and apps designed for beginners. Here are some popular options to consider:

• **Robinhood**: This app is beginner-friendly and allows you to start investing with as little as $1. It's perfect for those who want a simple, straightforward experience.

• **Fidelity** or **Charles Schwab**: These traditional brokerages offer more resources and tools, which can be helpful as you learn and grow as an investor.

• **Cash App**: Did you know you can buy stocks using this popular payment app? It's an easy way to dip your toes into investing without needing a separate account.

Most brokerages let you open an account online or through their app. You'll need to provide some basic information, like your name, address, Social Security number, and bank account details, to get started. Don't worry—this is a standard process, and your information is kept secure.

Step 3: Decide How Much to Invest

One of the most common questions beginners ask is, "How much money do I need to start investing?" The answer is: not much! Many brokerages allow you to buy fractional shares, which means you can invest as little as $5 or $10. For example, if a single share of Starbucks costs $100 and you only have $50, you can still buy half a share.

When deciding how much to invest, start small. Think of your first stock purchase as a learning experience. You're not trying to make a fortune overnight—you're dipping your toes into the market and getting comfortable with how it works. As you gain confidence and knowledge, you can always invest more.

Step 4: Research the Company

Once your brokerage account is set up and you've decided how much to invest, it's time to choose the company you want to invest in. This is where your knowledge of businesses you know and love comes in handy. Let's say you've decided to invest in Starbucks because you love their coffee and see how busy their stores are.

Start by doing a little research about the company. You don't need to dive into complex financial statements, but you should understand a few key things:

- **What does the company do?** Starbucks sells coffee and other beverages, but they also make money from food, merchandise, and partnerships.

- **How long has the company been around?** Established companies with a strong history are often more stable investments.

- **Is the company growing?** Check to see if Starbucks is opening new locations or introducing new products, which could signal future growth.

Many brokerage platforms provide basic information about each company, including a summary of what they do, recent news, and stock performance. You can also visit the company's website or read news articles to learn more.

Step 5: Search for the Stock

Now that you've chosen your company, it's time to find their stock on your brokerage platform. Every company has a unique stock ticker symbol, which is a short abbreviation used to identify their shares on the market. For example:

- Starbucks: **SBUX**
- McDonald's: **MCD**
- Dutch Bros Coffee: **BROS**

Use the search bar in your brokerage app to type in the

company name or ticker symbol. Once you find the stock, click on it to view details like the current price, historical performance, and any recent updates.

Step 6: Place Your Order

When you're ready to buy, you'll need to decide what type of order to place. Don't let this part intimidate you—it's simpler than it sounds. Here are the two most common types of orders:

• **Market Order**: This means you'll buy the stock at its current price. If Starbucks is trading at $100 per share, your market order will purchase it at that price.

• **Limit Order**: This lets you set a maximum price you're willing to pay. For example, if you want to buy Starbucks stock but only if it drops to $95, you can set a limit order.

For your first stock purchase, a market order is usually the easiest option.

Once you've chosen your order type, enter the amount you want to invest. If you're buying fractional shares, you can simply enter a dollar amount, like $50. Then click "Buy" to complete your purchase.

Step 7: Celebrate—You're Now a Shareholder!

Congratulations! You've officially bought your first stock.

Take a moment to celebrate this milestone—it's a big step toward building your financial future. As a shareholder, you now own a small piece of the company, and you'll benefit from its success over time.

Step 8: Monitor Your Investment

After buying your stock, it's natural to want to check the price constantly. But resist the urge to obsess over daily fluctuations. Stock prices go up and down all the time, and these short-term changes don't always reflect the company's true value.

Instead, focus on the bigger picture. Keep an eye on the company itself—are their stores still busy? Are they launching new products or opening new locations? These real-world indicators are often more reassuring than the numbers on your screen.

Step 9: Hold for the Long Term

One of the best strategies for new investors is to hold onto your stock for the long term. Successful companies like Starbucks or McDonald's have grown steadily over the years, rewarding investors who stayed patient. By holding onto your stock through the market's ups and downs, you give your investment time to grow.

Buying your first stock is an exciting and empowering experience. By following these steps and starting with a company you know and believe in, you're setting yourself up for success. Remember, investing is a journey—take your time, keep learning, and enjoy the ride!

Chapter 8
Unlocking Doors to New Opportunities

John sat in the driver's seat of his truck, the engine humming softly around him. The sun was getting lower, and its light stretched across the dashboard. As each mile passed, John thought about how he could use these quiet hours better. The road ahead seemed to go on forever, but it also felt like it kept him stuck in the same pattern of stops and starts.

He remembered talking to an old high school friend who used short breaks to do big things—buying stocks during coffee breaks, learning new languages between meetings. John's grip on the wheel got tighter as he wondered: could he use his own free moments to reach bigger goals? The idea made him feel excited and nervous at the same time.

At the next rest stop, John opened his laptop and searched for online classes. The computer's glow lit up the dark around him. He found courses about coding, handling money, and even starting a business. Each one seemed to promise a chance to grow and change. He felt pulled in two directions: the safe world he knew and this new world of learning and new skills.

What if he could learn to use his time so well that it gave him more than just miles on the road? Could these small moments add up to something big, like new skills and greater freedom?

Unlock the Power of Every Minute

Time is one of the most precious things you have. For truck drivers, time can feel tricky because our work schedule often changes. Learning how to use your time well isn't just about following a plan. It's about turning small breaks into chances to learn new skills and earn more money.

As a truck driver, you spend many hours on the road. This can make your life feel a bit messy. But that same life gives you special chances, too. If you manage your time well, you can find moments to learn and grow, right in the middle of your busy day.

You don't need to find big blocks of time to learn. Instead, look for smaller bits of time and use them wisely. Maybe you listen to a helpful podcast while you drive. Maybe you plan your money goals during your rest stops. Every minute can count if you know how to use it.

Learning Wherever You Go

Today, it's easy to learn online. Many websites and apps let you learn new things when you want. That means you can study business, money tips, or other skills even while on the road. You can learn in small bits—perfect for someone always on the move.

Good time management is about more than just filling up your day. It means deciding what is most important to you. Maybe you choose to spend a few minutes each day studying a new skill. Maybe you set aside a certain time each week to plan your finances. These small steps add up over time.

By using your time wisely, you can grow your skills and build a better future. You will learn to make every hour count. This can help you reach your money goals and set you on a path to a better life.

In this chapter, we'll dive deeper into practical techniques that help you harness every moment effectively. From choosing the right online courses that align with your career ambitions to strategically planning your weeks, you will learn how small increments of organized time can lead to significant achievements.

By embracing these strategies, you not only enhance your professional life but also set a foundation for success that transcends your current role on the road. Let's embark on this journey together—transforming every second on the clock into a stepping stone towards achieving your financial dreams.

Time Management Techniques for Truck Drivers

Using your time well is very important, especially if you are a truck driver. Because you spend long hours on the road and don't always know what your day will bring, good time management can help you get more done and feel better about your work. Simple steps, like planning your breaks, setting goals you can reach each day, and using helpful tools for planning routes, can make a big difference.

Think of each day like a delivery route. You would carefully plan where to go and in what order. In the same way, you can plan how to use your time. You can set aside time for work tasks, rest, and even learning new skills. Doing this helps you stay fresh and keeps you from feeling too tired or stressed.

There are many tools, such as apps and digital planners, made just for truck drivers. These can help you keep track of your hours, plan your path, and remember when things need to get done. They act like helpers you carry in your pocket, making it easier to manage your day.

Because your schedule can change a lot, you may need to be flexible. Maybe you set different goals when plans shift or decide which tasks are most important first. Every driver is different, so find a plan that fits your life.

Good time management isn't just about getting more work done. It also helps you grow as a person and enjoy your time on the road. By using these ideas, you can keep moving toward your job goals and still have time for yourself.

Discovering Online Learning Platforms

In today's digital age, education is more accessible than ever, and for truck drivers, this is no exception. Online learning platforms offer a variety of courses that can be tailored to fit the sporadic schedules of truckers. Platforms like Coursera, Udemy, and Khan Academy provide flexible learning options that drivers can access from anywhere, at any time, whether during a rest stop or at home.

These platforms cover a vast range of topics, from business management and investment to health and wellness. This diversity allows truck drivers to explore new interests or enhance existing skills that can contribute to their career growth and financial independence. The key is to choose courses that offer self-paced learning and do not require simultaneous online presence, catering perfectly to the unpredictable nature of life on the road.

Imagine transforming the cab of your truck into a personal classroom. This analogy underscores the transformational power of online learning, turning idle time into productive and enriching moments. The courses not only provide knowledge but also the flexibility needed to accommodate a trucker's lifestyle.

With advancements in mobile technology and the widespread availability of the internet, the barriers to accessing education have significantly diminished. Truck drivers now have the potential to become continuous learners, which not only enhances their skills but also opens doors to new career opportunities beyond trucking.

Prioritizing and Organizing Time

For truck drivers who want more than just the open road, using time wisely is very important. It's about making each minute count. By setting clear goals and picking certain times for learning or planning, you can use your free moments to build a brighter future beyond driving.

Think of time management like loading a truck. You need to put things in the right places so the weight is balanced. In the same way, your time should be split between work, learning new things, and enjoying life. When you balance your time, you can get more done without feeling too busy or stressed.

Starting new projects or learning new skills takes a plan. You might pick a certain time each day or week just for this. Maybe you learn about stocks, real estate, or how to start your own business. By following a set schedule, you stay focused and make real progress.

A time management expert named Laura Vanderkam once said that when you plan your week, you make sure you have time for what matters most. This idea works well for truck drivers, whose work hours may change, but whose goals stay the same.

Good time management, easy online classes, and time to improve yourself can lead you to new opportunities and more money. It's not just about following a clock—it's about unlocking doors to learning and earning. As a truck driver, your day may not be normal, but these tips are made just for you. Use your spare moments to learn something new online or plan your future. Every short break at a truck stop or waiting time at a shipper can be used to learn, grow, and plan. The main idea is simple: use your time wisely so you can be free and stable with your money later.

Ask yourself: Are you using your downtime in the best way? Could you fit learning into your daily life? Doing so can help your mind stay active, reduce stress, and give you the joy of reaching your goals.

Picture what can happen when you start using these time management ideas. You might build better skills, find new types of work, and change your whole life path. It's not just about your job—it's about making your life better.

Stick with it, and don't give up. Getting good at time management takes practice, but every small step helps you gain more freedom and safety for your future. Keep your eyes on what you want, stay curious, and keep moving forward. One day, you'll look back and be glad you invested this time in yourself. Keep on rolling toward a brighter, safer tomorrow.

Chapter 9

Expanding Your Professional Reach

Jim had always considered the rumble of his truck as the heartbeat of his life. Now, parked outside a small diner just off Interstate 70, he stared at his smartphone — a device that felt more foreign than familiar in his hands. He was attempting to navigate LinkedIn, a platform as alien to him as the cities he had merely passed through.

The sun was setting, casting long shadows that stretched across the asphalt like fingers trying to pull him back into the cab. Inside the diner, the clatter of dishes and murmur of conversations created a comforting backdrop. Jim remembered conversations with younger drivers, talking about opportunities beyond trucking — tech jobs, logistics management, even sales. They spoke of networking like it was second nature; for Jim, it felt like learning a new language.

He recalled advice from an old friend who had made a similar transition. "It's about who you know and who knows you," his friend had said. That simple idea seemed daunting in its simplicity. How could years behind the wheel translate to something valuable in this new digital age? His mind wandered to days when job changes meant hitting the road for new towns with better pay per mile, not crafting digital profiles highlighting professional strengths.

A waitress stepped outside for a breath of fresh air, her laughter briefly pulling him from his thoughts. She noticed his furrowed brow and offered a sympathetic smile before retreating back inside. The warmth of her gesture reminded him that connections were human at their core; perhaps he could navigate this new world with the same intuition that had guided him through millions of miles on the open road.

As night fell, Jim's doubts mingled with resolve. Was it

possible for someone so accustomed to tangible horizons to thrive in virtual landscapes? Could he extend his network beyond familiar faces at truck stops and into offices and boardrooms?

How might others help guide him through these uncharted territories?

Is Your Network Working for You?

Networking is not just about exchanging business cards or adding connections on social media; it's about building bridges to new opportunities that stretch well beyond the familiar horizons of truck driving. As you contemplate life after the truck, understanding the power of a robust professional network can be your strongest ally in transitioning to a new career path.

The Power of Virtual Handshakes

In today's digital age, building and maintaining a professional network remotely has become more than just a possibility—it's a potent strategy. The shift towards online networking platforms offers an unprecedented opportunity to connect with professionals across various industries. This can be particularly advantageous if you're looking to diversify your career options. Learning **how to effectively navigate these digital spaces** can provide you with insights and opportunities that were previously out of reach, ensuring that you're not just a participant but a competitor in the new industry you choose to enter.

Exploring New Territories

The traditional trucking community offers comfort and familiarity but stepping outside this circle can open up numerous doors. Platforms like LinkedIn are not just tools; they are gateways to communities that can offer invaluable advice, mentorship, and even job opportunities in fields you might not have considered before. Engaging with these platforms allows you to showcase your skills, making it clear that your talents extend far beyond the driver's seat.

Turning Connections into Opportunities

Identifying and utilizing key platforms is only part of the equation; the real magic happens when you leverage these connections to propel yourself into new career dimensions. Networking is not merely about collecting contacts but about cultivating meaningful relationships that can lead to real career opportunities. Through thoughtful engagement and consistent communication, these relationships can open up pathways into industries that need your unique skills.

It's imperative to approach networking with an open mind and a strategic plan. By broadening your professional circle, you're not only gaining access to job leads but also tapping into a wealth of knowledge and experience that can help smooth your transition into new professional arenas.

Envisioning Your Future Beyond the Wheel

Imagine a future where your daily commute could be as simple as walking to your home office, or where your knowledge of logistics and transportation opens up consulting opportunities. This isn't just wishful thinking—it's a potential reality with effective networking.

By engaging with individuals from diverse backgrounds, you gain insights into how different industries operate, which can spark innovative ideas for your own ventures or make you an attractive candidate for new sectors looking for someone with your expertise.

Embrace this journey with optimism and persistence, recognizing that each interaction could lead to substantial growth and learning. This proactive approach will not only expand your professional landscape but also enhance your personal growth, making the transition from truck driving to another career path both successful and fulfilling.

Remember: every conversation is a doorway to a new opportunity; make sure you're ready to step through it whenever it opens!

Building and Maintaining a Professional

Network Remotely

Building a professional network remotely is like planting a garden in your backyard. You start with a few seeds (connections) and with consistent care and interaction, these can grow into valuable relationships that bear fruit (opportunities). For truck drivers looking to expand their career horizons, understanding the art of remote networking is crucial. It allows you to connect with industry leaders, mentors, and peers beyond your immediate environment, without the constraints of geographical boundaries.

The first step in cultivating this digital network is to create a compelling online presence. Platforms like LinkedIn serve as the soil where your professional seeds can be sown. A well-crafted profile that highlights your experiences, skills, and aspirations acts as fertile ground for connections to take root. Regular updates and active engagement with content relevant to your new career interests help in nurturing these growing connections.

Imagine your online network as a web. Each strand represents a connection, and the strength of the web depends on how well you maintain these connections. This involves more than just adding people to your network; it's about engaging with them, sharing insights, and offering value. Regularly commenting on posts, sharing articles, and participating in discussions can establish your presence and credibility within the network.

Utilizing tools like virtual meetings and webinars can further solidify these connections. Just as you would attend industry conferences and workshops, these online events offer similar opportunities for learning and interacting, but from the comfort of your truck or home. They provide a platform to ask questions, exchange ideas, and even collaborate on projects, despite physical distances.

Effective remote networking is about consistently nurturing relationships with meaningful interactions and a strong online presence.

Key Platforms for Networking

When it comes to networking, not all platforms are created equal, especially for those transitioning out of traditional trucking roles. LinkedIn is undoubtedly a powerhouse for professional connections, but other platforms like Twitter and industry-specific forums also offer unique advantages. Twitter, for instance, allows for real-time engagement with industry leaders through simple tweets or direct messages, providing a less formal but often more immediate way to connect.

Think of LinkedIn as a professional suit, ideal for interviews and formal meetings, while Twitter is more like business casual, perfect for more informal, yet potentially impactful, interactions. These platforms complement each other, allowing you to tailor your approach based on the context and the type of connection you're looking to establish.

Exploring niche forums and online communities specific to your areas of interest in new careers can also be incredibly beneficial. These forums often house discussions on the latest trends, challenges, and opportunities in specific sectors. Participating in these conversations not only boosts your knowledge but also puts you in direct contact with potential mentors who can provide guidance and support as you navigate your career transition.

A lesser-known but equally important tool is Slack. Many professional groups and communities use Slack channels to share information and network. By joining these channels, you can tap into a concentrated pool of professionals and enthusiasts who share your interests.

For those who are less tech-savvy, starting with one platform and gradually expanding your digital footprint can help in managing the learning curve without becoming overwhelmed. Each platform has its unique rhythm and learning to navigate them effectively is key to maximizing your networking efforts.

How might embracing these platforms open doors to

opportunities you've never considered before?

Utilizing Networking to Find Opportunities

Networking is not just about building connections; it's about leveraging these relationships to open up new career pathways. For truck drivers exploring new industries, a robust network can be the key to uncovering opportunities that are not advertised or accessible through traditional job applications.

Consider your network as a radar system, constantly scanning the environment for opportunities. The more extensive your network, the larger your radar's reach, and the better your chances of detecting exciting career opportunities. Engaging actively with your connections can provide you with insights about upcoming opportunities, recommendations, and referrals, which are often crucial in career transitions.

Expanding your network across diverse industries can also offer a broader perspective, helping you understand where your skills could be best applied outside of trucking. This broadened view can reveal career paths you may not have considered, from logistics management to supply chain consulting, where your trucking experience offers valuable insights.

One effective strategy is informational interviewing. This

involves reaching out to individuals in your desired field for informal conversations. These interactions can provide a deeper understanding of the industry and help you identify how to position yourself for a career shift. Each informational interview not only expands your knowledge but also your network, incrementally improving your radar.

Networking is a powerful tool for discovering new career opportunities. By building a broad and engaged network, you can uncover paths that align with your skills and aspirations, ensuring a smoother transition into exciting new professional arenas.

As we wrap up our exploration of expanding your professional reach, remember that the journey doesn't end within the confines of trucking alone. By harnessing the power of remote networking, exploring platforms beyond traditional trucking communities, and leveraging these connections for career diversification, you open doors to numerous possibilities that extend far beyond the open road.

Building and maintaining a professional network remotely is not just beneficial; it's essential in today's digital age. Platforms like LinkedIn are more than just social sites; they are springboards into pools of opportunities and knowledge across various industries. Engaging with these platforms allows you to tap into a wealth of advice and insights, significantly broadening your career prospects.

The key is not just to build connections but to nurture them with the same diligence you would apply to maintaining your rig. Regular updates, participating in discussions, and sharing your experiences can turn distant online contacts into robust professional relationships. This proactive approach in **networking can be your most reliable navigator** as you chart a new course in your career.

Consider this: every interaction you have is a potential lead to a new career path or business venture. By stepping outside the traditional trucking forums and engaging with people from diverse fields, you not only gain insights into other industries but also set the stage for possible collaborations that could translate into passive income streams.

What new opportunities can you discover today? Who in your network can introduce you to a completely different field? These questions are not just thought experiments—they are practical steps towards **utilizing networking for discovering a new career.**

Embrace the challenge with optimism. Transitioning to a new career is no small feat, but with a solid network and a willingness to learn and adapt, your potential is limitless. The roads you drive now are just part of a larger map—one that includes paths you might never have considered if not for your willingness to connect and grow professionally.

Take these insights and use them as a guide as you navigate towards financial freedom and career fulfillment. Each connection you make is not just a potential job or a business opportunity—it's a step towards a richer, more diversified professional life.

Remember, the road to riches is not just paved with hard work but with smart, strategic networking. Let's drive forward, not just on highways but across the vast network of opportunities that await

Chapter 10
Teaching and Mentoring

Miles, a seasoned truck driver, was guiding his big rig along the curvy backroads of Pennsylvania. The sun was dipping low in the sky, painting everything with warm shades of orange and purple. The colors danced on his dashboard as the truck rumbled along, but Miles wasn't paying much attention to the beauty outside. His mind was stuck on a conversation he'd had earlier at a truck stop with a young driver named Leo.

Leo had been full of questions—how to handle icy roads, how to squeeze a big rig into tight city spaces. They were the kinds of things Miles had learned the hard way over decades of driving. He had answered Leo's questions as best he could, but now, as the miles rolled by, he couldn't stop thinking about it. Every mile he'd driven, every challenge he'd faced, had taught him something. What if he could take all those lessons and pass them on to drivers like Leo? Could teaching be the next road for him to travel?

As the truck's engine hummed steadily, his thoughts grew louder. He remembered his early days—the steep learning curve, the near-misses on icy highways, and the times he'd had to rely on pure instinct to get out of a tricky spot. Each moment had shaped him into the driver he was today.

What if he could share those stories? Not just the how-to's of trucking, but the deeper wisdom behind them—the kind of lessons you only learn by living through them.

The radio crackled with a weather report, but Miles barely noticed. He was lost in thought. He pictured himself standing in front of a group of young drivers, explaining how to read the road, trust their instincts, and handle the unexpected. The idea made his chest feel a little lighter, like maybe he was onto something.

Changing Lanes

As he pulled up to a red light, Miles watched families in cars passing by, kids in the back seats, music playing. He thought about his own family—how much he missed seeing them grow up, how most of their time together was crammed into holidays and short breaks between hauls. What if teaching meant he could be home more often? The thought stirred something in him, a mixture of hope and longing.

A few miles later, he took an exit that led to an old diner he knew well. It was a popular stop for truckers, a place where the coffee was hot and the stories flowed freely. He parked under the big oak tree in the corner of the lot, its branches swaying gently in the evening breeze. Miles leaned back in his seat and stared up at the leaves. It almost felt like they were whispering to him, sharing their own quiet stories about seasons of change.

Could his years on the road, all those hard-earned lessons, become a roadmap for others? Could he help new drivers steer clear of the mistakes he'd made? Maybe, just maybe, his journey wasn't just about moving freight from one place to another. Maybe it was about finding a way to guide others, to make their roads a little less bumpy.

As Miles stepped down from his truck and walked toward the diner, the idea stayed with him. Sharing his knowledge, his stories—maybe that was his next destination. It wasn't just about where he'd been, but where he could go from here. And maybe, just maybe, it could make the miles ahead feel even more meaningful.

Transforming Miles into Mentorship

In the dynamic world of trucking, each mile on the road isn't just a measure of distance—it's an accumulation of valuable experiences and lessons. As a truck driver, you've navigated through countless challenges, adapting to diverse scenarios that have honed your skills and deepened your understanding of the industry. Now, imagine channeling this rich repository of knowledge into a powerful tool for financial growth and professional evolution. This chapter delves into how your personal journey can transition from practical experience to influential teaching and mentoring roles within the trucking community and beyond.

The Roadmap to Sharing Wisdom

Embarking on this transformative journey begins with **documenting your unique experiences**. Every truck driver's story is a blend of technical know-how, real-life problem solving, and adaptability—qualities that are immensely valuable in educational content. Whether it's mastering ELDs, understanding the intricacies of engine maintenance, or navigating the regulatory landscapes across states, your day-to-day encounters offer a real-world curriculum ripe for sharing.

Mentorship: Steering Novices to Mastery

The leap from driver to mentor involves more than just sharing knowledge; it requires cultivating trust and demonstrating proven success in the field. As mentors, seasoned drivers like you can provide not only guidance but also inspiration to those just starting their careers or facing hurdles similar to what you've overcome. Establishing yourself as a mentor is about **building relationships** based on respect and genuine interest in helping others grow.

Educational Courses and Books: From Concept to Classroom

The digital age offers unprecedented opportunities for creating structured learning pathways from your experiences. Online courses and instructional books allow you to reach a broader audience eager to learn about truck driving tactics, safety protocols, and efficiency enhancements. This segment explores how these tools not only contribute to your income but also elevate your professional profile significantly.

Connecting Chapters: A Recap of Your Journey

Reflecting on the earlier discussions in this book—from

investing in real estate as a passive income stream to leveraging digital platforms for brand building—this chapter ties all these elements together under the umbrella of education and mentorship. It emphasizes how teaching others not only solidifies your own understanding but also establishes you as an authority figure in the industry.

By transforming your firsthand experiences into educational content or mentorship programs, you are not merely passing on knowledge; you are enhancing your own career prospects and financial stability. This transition opens new doors, enabling roles in training, coaching, or consulting that may extend well beyond traditional trucking paths.

As we approach the end of our guide, remember that each strategy discussed is a step towards securing a future where financial freedom is not just a destination but a journey made richer through sharing your knowledge and guiding others. Embrace this opportunity to influence and inspire as you steer toward new horizons beyond the truck.

Explore Ways to Document and Share Personal Trucking Experiences

Truck drivers accumulate a vast array of experiences on the road, each one a potential lesson or story that could benefit others. Documenting these experiences is the first step toward sharing this valuable knowledge. Using simple tools like journals, blogs, or video diaries, drivers can capture the details of their journeys, including the challenges they face and the solutions they devise.

Imagine your trucking career as a vast landscape filled with unique landmarks. Each landmark represents a significant experience or insight. Documenting these is like creating a map for others to follow, preventing them from getting lost in similar situations. It's not just about where you traveled, but about what you learned along the way.

Moreover, these documented experiences can be transformed into educational content. For instance, a blog post about handling unexpected weather conditions becomes a lesson in safety preparedness. Similarly, a video explaining a particularly efficient route can save others time and fuel. The key is to make the content relatable and easy to understand, focusing on practical advice that fellow drivers can apply in their own careers.

Digital platforms offer an expansive audience for this content. Social media, trucking forums, and dedicated websites allow drivers to share their stories and advice far and wide. Engaging with the audience through comments and discussions can also provide feedback, helping to refine the content and make it even more useful.

Documenting and sharing trucking experiences not only

preserves valuable insights but also connects the community, enhancing everyone's knowledge.

Establishing Yourself as a Mentor or Coach

With a wealth of experience behind the wheel, seasoned truck drivers are uniquely equipped to guide newcomers through the intricacies of the trucking profession. Establishing oneself as a mentor or coach involves more than just offering advice; it requires a structured approach to teaching and a genuine desire to help others succeed.

Mentorship in trucking can take various forms, from informal advice shared over coffee to formal training sessions. The first step is often to identify what you are uniquely qualified to teach. Whether it's navigating through tricky terrains, managing long haul fatigue, or optimizing fuel usage, your specialized knowledge is invaluable.

Creating a mentorship program can be likened to building a bridge. Just as a bridge connects two previously separate points, mentorship connects experience with inexperience, creating a pathway for knowledge transfer. This bridge not only helps new drivers but also reinforces the mentor's own understanding and skills.

Effective mentors are approachable and empathetic, traits that encourage mentees to engage openly and learn comfortably. Moreover, mentors need to be patient and adaptable, ready to adjust their teaching methods to meet varied learning styles and needs.

To promote your services, consider partnerships with trucking schools or local transport companies. These collaborations can help you reach potential mentees. Additionally, maintaining a presence on relevant online forums and social media groups can increase your visibility within the trucking community.

How can your unique journey and insights pave the way for others in the trucking industry?

Creating Online Courses or Writing Instructional Books

The trucking industry is ripe with opportunities for those willing to share their expertise through formal educational products like online courses or instructional books. These resources can help aspiring and current truck drivers not only perform their duties more efficiently but also advance in their careers.

Creating an online course allows you to structure your knowledge into digestible modules, which students can progress through at their own pace. It's crucial to include interactive elements such as quizzes, discussion boards, and practical exercises. These components encourage active learning and help reinforce the material.

Consider the process of creating an online course as assembling a toolkit. Each tool you include is designed to address specific challenges or tasks that truck drivers face daily. Your course should equip them with everything they need to navigate the complexities of their job confidently.

Writing a book, on the other hand, allows for deeper dives into topics. It can be a comprehensive guide covering everything from the basics of truck maintenance to advanced driving techniques. The key to success is ensuring the information is both accurate and accessible, with plenty of real-life examples and simple explanations.

Whether you choose to create a course, write a book, or both, these platforms can significantly amplify your impact in the trucking community. By formalizing your knowledge, you not only establish yourself as an expert but also create a lasting resource that can benefit countless individuals.

By documenting experiences, engaging as mentors, and creating educational products, truck drivers can significantly influence the next generation of road warriors.

Throughout this chapter, we've explored how your journey as a truck driver can pivot towards impactful roles in teaching and mentoring. By documenting and sharing your personal experiences, you not only preserve valuable knowledge but also set the stage for becoming a trusted mentor or coach. The road doesn't end with driving; it extends into guiding others on their own paths through your insights and expertise.

Transforming your trucking journey into educational content offers a dual benefit. It not only enhances your professional profile but also opens up new income streams. Whether through online courses, instructional books, or personalized coaching sessions, the knowledge you impart can significantly impact the lives of upcoming drivers and the industry at large. This transition is more than a career shift—it's a way to leave a legacy.

The broader themes of this book emphasize the importance of diversifying income and preparing for future shifts in the trucking industry. From real estate investments to digital content creation, the strategies discussed are designed to equip you with the tools to achieve financial freedom and career fulfillment. **Your experience on the road is invaluable**, and when channeled effectively, it can lead to prosperous avenues beyond traditional truck driving.

I encourage you to view these opportunities not just as alternatives, but as enhancements to your career trajectory. The potential for growth and development is immense, and with the right approach, your transition can be both seamless and rewarding. Consider what aspects of your experience could serve as learning material, and take proactive steps towards building those into your new career path.

Remember, every mile you've driven has equipped you with unique skills and insights. Now, it's about steering those experiences towards new horizons where you can continue to make a significant impact. Embrace this journey with optimism, and let your legacy in the trucking industry be as a pioneer who not only navigated the roads but also paved new ones for others to follow.

As we wrap up, reflect on how each chapter has built upon the last, culminating in a comprehensive guide to not just surviving but thriving in a changing landscape. Your road to riches is paved with the knowledge you now hold; drive forward with confidence and determination.

Epilogue

A Final Word on Financial Freedom and Career Transformation

As we wrap up this journey together, it's essential to reflect on the powerful insights and strategies we've explored. This book has been crafted not just as a guide but as a companion in your quest for a life beyond the truck. It's about breaking free from the constraints of the road and steering toward a future rich with possibilities and security.

We've delved into the world of real estate investment, uncovering how properties can serve as stepping stones to financial independence. **Digital marketing and content creation** have opened doors to personal branding and passive income, transforming your unique trucking experiences into engaging stories that resonate with audiences worldwide.

Stock investments have been demystified, showing you how to make the market work for you, even from behind the wheel. And perhaps most crucially, we've explored how becoming a driver recruiter can not only increase your income but also give back to the industry that has been your home for years.

The practical applications of these strategies are vast. Each chapter was designed to be actionable, allowing you to start small and scale up as your confidence and resources grow. Whether it's setting aside two hours a week to learn about stocks or using layovers to produce engaging content for your new YouTube channel, the steps have been laid out for you to follow.

Yet, as comprehensive as this guide is, it's important to acknowledge its limitations. The landscape of digital marketing is ever-evolving, and real estate markets fluctuate. Continuous learning will be your best tool in adapting to these changes. I encourage you to keep exploring, keep questioning, and most importantly, keep taking action.

Take these lessons and adapt them to fit your life. Maybe you'll find a niche in the digital world that speaks directly to truckers like yourself or discover an untapped real estate market in towns you frequent on your routes. The key is to use what you've learned here as a foundation upon which you can build a more secure and fulfilling future.

In closing, remember that change is not just possible; it's within reach. You hold the map now; where you go next is up to you.

"The only impossible journey is the one you never begin." — Tony Robbins

www.ingramcontent.com/pod-product-compliance
Lightning Source LLC
Chambersburg PA
CBHW031420210526
45464CB00005B/1970